BIG IDEAS

MATH.

Skills Review and
Basic Skills Handbook

BIG IDEAS
LEARNING.

Erie, Pennsylvania
BigIdeasLearning.com

Big Ideas Learning, LLC
1762 Norcross Road
Erie, PA 16510-3838
USA

For product information and customer support, contact Big Ideas Learning
at **1-877-552-7766** or visit us at ***BigIdeasLearning.com***.

Printed in the U.S.A.

ISBN 13: 978-1-60840-155-0
ISBN 10: 1-60840-155-3

4 5 6 7 8 9 10 VLP 14 13 12

SKILLS REVIEW HANDBOOK

The Skills Review Handbook provides examples and practice to review concepts from earlier grades.

BASIC SKILLS HANDBOOK

The Basic Skills Handbook offers a simplified, more visual approach to understanding concepts from earlier grades.

SKILLS REVIEW HANDBOOK

BASIC SKILLS HANDBOOK

SKILLS REVIEW HANDBOOK

REVIEW: Rounding Whole Numbers

Name _____

Key Concept and Vocabulary

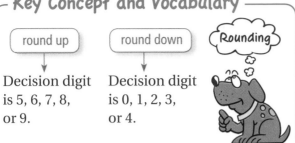

round up → Decision digit is 5, 6, 7, 8, or 9.

round down → Decision digit is 0, 1, 2, 3, or 4.

Rounding

Visual Model

To round to the *nearest ten,* choose the closest multiple of ten.

27 is closer to 30 than to 20. So, 27 rounds to 30.

Skill Examples

1. To the *nearest ten:*
   113 rounds to 110.

2. To the *nearest hundred:*
   182 rounds to 200.

3. To the *nearest thousand:*
   4506 rounds to 5000.

Application Example

4. An appraiser adds the areas of the rooms in a house and gets 1548 square feet. Estimate this to the nearest ten square feet.

   To the *nearest ten:* 1548 rounds to 1550.

   The house has about 1550 square feet.

PRACTICE MAKES PURR-FECT™

Check your answers at BigIdeasMath.com.

Round to the nearest ten. (The symbol ≈ means "is approximately equal to.")

5. 57 ≈ _____

6. 142 ≈ _____

7. 345 ≈ _____

8. 189 ≈ _____

Round to the nearest hundred.

9. 57 ≈ _____

10. 142 ≈ _____

11. 345 ≈ _____

12. 189 ≈ _____

Round to the nearest thousand.

13. 23,450 ≈ _____

14. 3623 ≈ _____

15. 872 ≈ _____

16. 45,214 ≈ _____

Round the area of the figure to the nearest ten.

17.
86 ft²

Area ≈ _____

18.
124 cm²

Area ≈ _____

19.
23 in.²

Area ≈ _____

20.
77 m²

Area ≈ _____

21. **NATIONAL DEBT** In February of 2009, the national debt for the United States was $10,770,358,064,879. Round this debt to the nearest billion dollars. _____

22. **POPULATION OF TEXAS** To the nearest thousand, the population of Texas was estimated to be 24,327,000 in 2008. Describe the actual population that Texas could have had in 2008.

REVIEW: Adding and Subtracting Whole Numbers

Name _____

Key Concept and Vocabulary

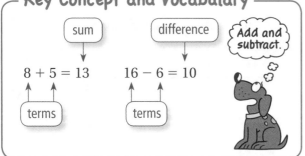

sum

$8 + 5 = 13$

terms

difference

$16 - 6 = 10$

terms

Add and subtract.

Visual Model

To add on a number line, move to the *right*.

$2 + 4 = 6$

To subtract on a number line, move to the *left*.

Skill Examples

1. $12 + 17 = 29$ **2.** $23 + 0 = 23$

3. $114 + 5 + 18 = 137$

4. $9 - 4 = 5$ **5.** $16 - 0 = 16$

6. $139 - 39 = 100$

Application Example

7. You spent $3 for socks, $28 for gym shoes, $18 for a T-shirt, and $15 for shorts. How much did you spend for your gym outfit?

$3 + 28 + 18 + 15 = 64$

∴ You spent $64.

PRACTICE MAKES PURR-FECT™

Check your answers at BigIdeasMath.com.

Find the sum or difference.

8. $21 + 7 =$ _____   **9.** $94 + 0 =$ _____   **10.** $104 + 142 =$ _____   **11.** $1147 + 234 =$ _____

12. $19 - 18 =$ _____   **13.** $39 - 29 =$ _____   **14.** $72 - 49 =$ _____   **15.** $1035 - 246 =$ _____

16. $941 - 0 =$ _____   **17.** $12 + 5 + 8 =$ _____   **18.** $31 + 1 + 1 =$ _____   **19.** $123 + 41 + 18 =$ ___

Find the perimeter of the rectangle or triangle.

20.
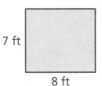
7 ft
8 ft

Perimeter = _____

21.
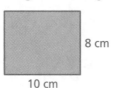
8 cm
10 cm

Perimeter = _____

22.

18 in.   18 in.
21 in.

Perimeter = _____

23.
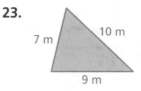
10 m
7 m
9 m

Perimeter = _____

24. RUNNING You ran 2 miles on Monday, 2 miles on Tuesday, 3 miles on Wednesday, 2 miles on Thursday, and 4 miles on Friday. How many miles did you run during the week? _____

25. PLANNING A SHOPPING TRIP You have $27 and take another $32 from your savings account. How much will you have left after buying a shirt for $18 and a pair of jeans for $29. Explain.

_____

_____

REVIEW: Multiplying Whole Numbers   Name _____

Key Concept and Vocabulary

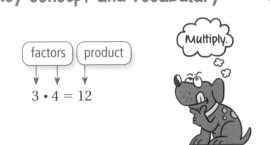

factors   product

$3 \cdot 4 = 12$

Visual Model

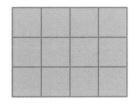

A rectangle that is 3 units by 4 units has an area of 12 square units.

Area $= 3 \times 4$

$= 12$ square units

Skill Examples

1. $6 \cdot 7 = 42$

2. $0 \times 5 = 0$

3. $8 \cdot 1 = 8$

4. $(9)(12) = 108$

5. $15 \times 20 = 300$

Application Example

6. Find the area of a rectangular lot that is 20 yards wide and 35 yards long.

   Area $=$ (length)(width)

   $= 35 \cdot 20$

   $= 700$ yd^2

   ⋮ The area is 700 square yards.

PRACTICE MAKES *PURR-FECT*™

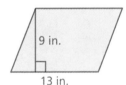

Check your answers at BigIdeasMath.com.

Find the product.

7. $8 \cdot 12 =$ _____

8. $15 \times 12 =$ _____

9. $(13)(20) =$ _____

10. $2 \cdot 240 =$ _____

11. $13 \times 6 =$ _____

12. $(11)(8) =$ _____

13. $19 \cdot 21 =$ _____

14. $30 \times 100 =$ _____

15. $0 \cdot 114 =$ _____

16. $26 \times 1 =$ _____

17. $4 \cdot 10 \cdot 8 =$ _____

18. $9 \cdot 14 \cdot 2 =$ _____

Find the area of the rectangle or parallelogram.

19.
5 ft
8 ft
Area = _____

20.
12 cm
7 cm
Area = _____

21.
9 in.
13 in.
Area = _____

22.
14 m
18 m
Area = _____

23. **SCHOOL BUS** Each school bus can carry a maximum of 50 passengers. What is the maximum number of passengers that 12 school buses can carry? _____

24. **PAPER CUPS** Each package contains 65 paper cups. You buy four packages. Do you have enough paper cups for 250 people to each have one? How do you know?

REVIEW: Dividing Whole Numbers

Name _____

Key Concept and Vocabulary

dividend   quotient

$10 \div 2 = 5$

divisor

Divide.

Visual Model

If you divide 6 units into 3 equal parts, each part will have 2 units.

| 2 units | 2 units | 2 units |

$6 \div 3 = 2$

Skill Examples

1. $42 \div 6 = 7$

2. $\dfrac{65}{13} = 65 \div 13 = 5$

3.
$$\begin{array}{r} 13 \\ 15\overline{)195} \\ 15 \\ \hline 45 \\ 45 \\ \hline 0 \end{array}$$

   $195 \div 15 = 13$

Application Example

4. Six people find a treasure worth $12,300. If each person receives an equal share, how much does each person get?

   $\$12,300 \div 6 = \$2050$

   Each person gets $2050.

PRACTICE MAKES *PURR-FECT*™

Check your answers at BigIdeasMath.com.

Find the quotient.

5. $56 \div 8 =$ _____

6. $99 \div 11 =$ _____

7. $132 \div 6 =$ _____

8. $80 \div 5 =$ _____

9. $\dfrac{88}{4} =$ _____

10. $\dfrac{156}{3} =$ _____

11. $\dfrac{430}{86} =$ _____

12. $\dfrac{3082}{23} =$ _____

13. $18\overline{)216}$

14. $12\overline{)960}$

15. $9\overline{)567}$

16. $19\overline{)323}$

Find the height of the rectangle or parallelogram.

17.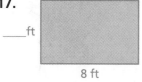
_____ft
8 ft
Area = 40 ft^2

18.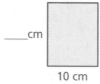
_____cm
10 cm
Area = 120 cm^2

19.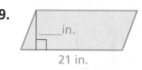
___ in.
21 in.
Area = 168 in.^{2}

20.
___ m
9 m
Area = 144 m^2

21. **PARTY PUNCH** A punch bowl contains 6 quarts of punch. There are 32 fluid ounces in a quart. How many 4-fluid ounce cups will the punch bowl serve? _____

22. **SHARING THE PROFIT** You and three friends start a small business. Your total income is $820 and your total expenses are $360. You share the profit evenly. How much do each of you get? Explain. _____

_____

REVIEW: Factors of Whole Numbers

Name _____

Key Concept and Vocabulary

Factors of 12: 1, 2, 3, 4, ⑥, 12

Factors of 18: 1, 2, 3, ⑥, 9, 18

↑

Greatest Common Factor

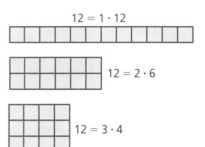

Factors

Visual Model

There are 3 ways to factor 12 into 2 whole numbers. Each way is represented by a rectangle.

$12 = 1 \cdot 12$

$12 = 2 \cdot 6$

$12 = 3 \cdot 4$

Skill Examples

1. Factors of 1: 1

2. Factors of 8: 1, 2, 4, 8

3. Factors of 7: 1, 7

4. Factors of 30: 1, 2, 3, 5, 6, 10, 15, 30

5. Factors of 33: 1, 3, 11, 33

Application Example

6. What is the greatest number of people with whom 20 pennies and 24 dimes can be shared so that each person gets the same share?

   The greatest common factor (GCF) of 20 and 24 is 4.

   ∴ The greatest number is 4 people.

PRACTICE MAKES *PURR*-FECT™

Check your answers at BigIdeasMath.com.

List all factors of both numbers. Then circle the greatest common factor.

7. Factors of 6: _____

   Factors of 9: _____

8. Factors of 8: _____

   Factors of 16: _____

9. Factors of 20: _____

   Factors of 30: _____

10. Factors of 75: _____

    Factors of 100: _____

11. Factors of 34: _____

    Factors of 51: _____

12. Factors of 10: _____

    Factors of 18: _____

13. Sketch all possible ways that 16 small squares can be arranged to form a rectangle.

14. **SHARING COINS** What is the greatest number of people with whom 30 nickels and 36 dimes can be shared so that each person gets the same share? _____

15. **DECK OF CARDS** A deck of cards has 52 cards. The deck can be divided into 4 piles of exactly 13 cards each. Describe all the other ways the deck can be divided into equal piles.

_____

_____

REVIEW: Divisibility Tests

Name _____

Key Concept and Vocabulary

A whole number is divisible by
- 2: if its last digit is 0, 2, 4, 6, or 8.
- 3: if the sum of the digits is divisible by 3.
- 4: if the number formed by the last two digits is divisible by 4.
- 5: if its last digit is 0 or 5.
- 6: if it is divisible by 2 and by 3.
- 9: if the sum of its digits is divisible by 9.

Skill Examples

1. 147 is divisible by 3 because
   $1 + 4 + 7 = 12$ is divisible by 3.

2. 524 is divisible by 4 because 24
   is divisible by 4.

3. 243 is divisible by 9 because
   $2 + 4 + 3 = 9$ is divisible by 9.

Application Example

4. There are 9 students in your class. Can
   you divide 839 stamps evenly, so that
   each student in your class gets the same
   number of stamps?

   The sum of the digits of 839 is
   $8 + 3 + 9 = 20$. 20 is not divisible by 9.

   No, you cannot divide the stamps evenly.

PRACTICE MAKES PURR-FECT™

Check your answers at BigIdeasMath.com.

Use a divisibility test to answer the question.

5. Is 146 divisible by 2? _____ 6. Is 153 divisible by 3? _____ 7. Is 378 divisible by 4? _____

8. Is 1255 divisible by 5? _____ 9. Is 147 divisible by 6? _____ 10. Is 333 divisible by 6? _____

11. Is 2769 divisible by 3? _____ 12. Is 5034 divisible by 3? _____ 13. Is 145 divisible by 15? _____

Decide whether x is a whole number. (Figures are not drawn to scale.)

14.
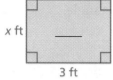
x ft
3 ft
Area = 87 ft^2

15.
x cm
9 cm
Area = 343 cm^2

16.
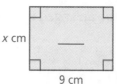
x in.
6 in.
Area = 256 in.^{2}

17.
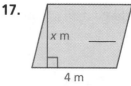
x m
4 m
Area = 144 m^2

18. **SHARING TIME** There are 360 minutes of monthly cell phone minutes for 4 people in a
    family. Can each person get the same number of minutes per month? If so, how many?

    _____

19. **CALENDAR** Assume that there are 365 days in a year. Describe the possible number of days
    in a week so that there is an exact number of weeks in a year. (*Hint: 7 is not one of them.*)

    _____

REVIEW: Prime and Composite Numbers

Name _____

Key Concept and Vocabulary

A **prime number** has only 1 and itself as factors. The first 5 prime numbers are 2, 3, 5, 7, and 11.

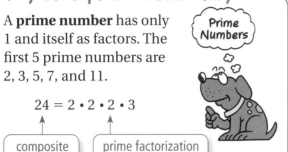

$$24 = 2 \cdot 2 \cdot 2 \cdot 3$$

composite ↑   ↑ prime factorization

Visual Model

You can use a **factor tree** to find the prime factorization of a composite number.

$$60 = 2 \cdot 2 \cdot 3 \cdot 5$$

Skill Examples

Prime Factorization

1. $30 = 2 \cdot 3 \cdot 5$

2. $42 = 2 \cdot 3 \cdot 7$

3. $81 = 3 \cdot 3 \cdot 3 \cdot 3$

4. $91 = 7 \cdot 13$

5. $89 = 89$ (Prime)

Application Example

6. You get a paycheck every 2 weeks. Your annual salary is \$30,000. Can you get the same amount for each paycheck?

$$30,000 = 2 \cdot 2 \cdot 2 \cdot 2 \cdot 3 \cdot 5 \cdot 5 \cdot 5 \cdot 5$$

∴ 30,000 is not divisible by 13, so you cannot have 26 paychecks of equal size.

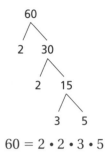

PRACTICE MAKES *PURR*-FECT™

Check your answers at BigIdeasMath.com.

Write the prime factorization of the number.

7. $45 =$ _____

8. $100 =$ _____

9. $63 =$ _____

10. $256 =$ _____

11. $54 =$ _____

12. $55 =$ _____

13. $121 =$ _____

14. $98 =$ _____

15. $113 =$ _____

16. Use a factor tree to find the prime factorization of 36.

17. **EQUAL PAYCHECKS** You get a paycheck every 2 weeks. Your annual salary is \$39,000. Can you get the same amount for each paycheck? Explain why or why not.

_____

_____

18. **LISTING PRIME NUMBERS** List all the prime numbers that are less than 50.

_____

REVIEW: Multiples of Whole Numbers

Name _____

Key Concept and Vocabulary

Multiples of 8:

   8, 16, 24, 32, (40,) 48, . . .

Multiples of 10:

   10, 20, 30, (40,) 50, . . .

least common multiple

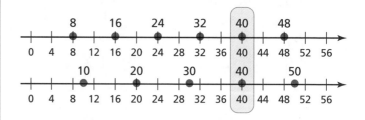

Visual Model

Skill Examples

1. The LCM of 4 and 6 is **12**.

2. The LCM of 1 and 3 is **3**.

3. The LCM of 3 and 5 is **15**. ◄— The LCM of two primes is their product.

4. The LCM of 12 and 40 is **120**.

5. The LCM of 11 and 33 is **33**.

Application Example

6. Find the minimum number of 6-taco packages that will serve 4 people with no tacos left over.

   The LCM of 4 and 6 is **12**.

   For 1 package, there will be 6 tacos and 2 will be left over. For 2 packages, there will be **12 tacos**. Each person gets 3.

PRACTICE MAKES PURR-FECT™

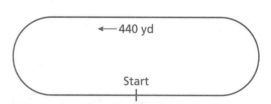

Check your answers at BigIdeasMath.com.

Find the least common multiple of the two whole numbers.

7. 3 and 7: _____

8. 3 and 6: _____

9. 6 and 9: _____

10. 9 and 12: _____

11. 6 and 21: _____

12. 24 and 30: _____

13. 24 and 32: _____

14. 15 and 40: _____

15. 48 and 128: _____

16. **RUNNING** One trip around a track is 440 yards. One runner can complete one lap in 8 minutes. Another can complete a lap in 6 minutes. How long will it take for both to arrive at the starting point together if they start at the same place? _____

←— 440 yd

Start

17. **BUYING TACOS** Find the minimum number of 5-taco packages that will serve 4 people with no tacos left over. How many will each person get?

_____

18. **HOW MANY PENNIES?** With the same collection of pennies, you can make stacks that have 3 pennies, 4 pennies, or 9 pennies with none left over. How many pennies do you have?

_____

REVIEW: Commutative and Associative Properties

Name _____

Key Concept and Vocabulary

Commutative Property
↓
$1 + 3 = 3 + 1$ *(Addition)*

$2 + (3 + 5) = (2 + 3) + 5$ *(Addition)*
↑
Associative Property

Commutative Property
↓
$2 \cdot 5 = 5 \cdot 2$ *(Multiplication)*

$2 \cdot (3 \cdot 5) = (2 \cdot 3) \cdot 5$ *(Multiplication)*
↑
Associative Property

Skill Examples

1. $3 + 6 = 6 + 3$

2. $15 + (5 + 3) = (15 + 5) + 3$

3. $4 \cdot 6 = 6 \cdot 4$

4. $2 \cdot (3 \cdot 5) = (2 \cdot 3) \cdot 5$

Application Example

5. Use the above properties and mental math to find the sum: $97 + 28 + 3 + 2$.

$97 + 28 + 3 + 2 = (97 + 3) + (28 + 2)$

$= 100 + 30$

$= 130$

The sum is 130.

PRACTICE MAKES *PURR*-FECT™

Check your answers at BigIdeasMath.com.

Identify the property. Then find the sum or product.

6. $11 + 36 = 36 + 11$ _____

7. $10 \cdot 4 = 4 \cdot 10$ _____

8. $5 \cdot (4 \cdot 2) = (5 \cdot 4) \cdot 2$ _____

9. $2 + (3 + 5) = (2 + 3) + 5$ _____

10. $2 + 3 + 4 = 2 + 4 + 3$ _____

11. $5 \cdot 2 \cdot 3 = 2 \cdot 5 \cdot 3$ _____

Show how you can use the Commutative and Associative Properties to find the sum or product using mental math.

12. $34 + 47 + 16 =$ _____

13. $5 \cdot 13 \cdot 2 =$ _____

14. $15 + 13 + 27 + 35 =$ _____

15. $9 \cdot 5 \cdot 3 \cdot 2 =$ _____

16. **COMMUTATIVITY** Describe two real-life activities that are *not* commutative. In other words, you get different results if you switch the order in which the activities are performed.

_____

REVIEW: Distributive Property

Name _____

Key Concept and Vocabulary

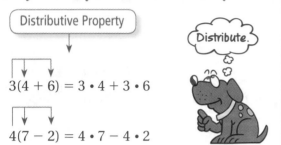

Distributive Property

$3(4 + 6) = 3 \cdot 4 + 3 \cdot 6$

$4(7 - 2) = 4 \cdot 7 - 4 \cdot 2$

Distribute.

Visual Model

$$2(3 + 5) \quad = \quad 2 \cdot 3 \quad + \quad 2 \cdot 5$$

Skill Examples

1. $3(9 + 4) = 3 \cdot 9 + 3 \cdot 4$

2. $7(10 - 3) = 7 \cdot 10 - 7 \cdot 3$

3. $6 \cdot 8 + 6 \cdot 7 = 6(8 + 7)$

4. $12 \cdot 9 - 12 \cdot 2 = 12(9 - 2)$

5. $5(2 + 5 + 3) = 5 \cdot 2 + 5 \cdot 5 + 5 \cdot 3$

Application Example

6. You buy 3 hot dogs for $1.25 each and 3 sodas for $0.75 each. Find the total cost.

$$3(1.25) + 3(0.75) = 3(1.25 + 0.75)$$
$$= 3(2.00)$$
$$= 6$$

⋮⋅ The total cost is $6.00.

PRACTICE MAKES *PURR*-FECT™

Check your answers at BigIdeasMath.com.

Use the Distributive Property to rewrite the expression.

7. $3(4 + 5) =$ _____

8. $5(8 - 3) =$ _____

9. $9(11 + 7) =$ _____

10. $8(27 - 9) =$ _____

11. $6(17 - 7) =$ _____

12. $4(7 + 3 + 2) =$ _____

13. $5 \cdot 7 + 5 \cdot 3$ _____

14. $2 \cdot 9 - 2 \cdot 6 =$ _____

15. $7 \cdot 4 + 7 \cdot 8 =$ _____

16.

17.

18. **MENTAL MATH** You buy 5 hot dogs for $1.29 each and 5 sodas for $0.71 each. Show how you can use mental math to find the total cost.

_____

19. **EXTENSION** Does the Distributive Property apply to a combination of addition *and* subtraction? Decide using the expression $3(7 + 5 - 4)$.

_____

REVIEW: Exponents

Name _____

Skill Examples

1. $3^2 = 3 \cdot 3 = 9$

2. $2^4 = 2 \cdot 2 \cdot 2 \cdot 2 = 16$

3. $4^3 = 4 \cdot 4 \cdot 4 = 64$

4. $5^4 = 5 \cdot 5 \cdot 5 \cdot 5 = 625$

5. $9^5 = 9 \cdot 9 \cdot 9 \cdot 9 \cdot 9 = 59{,}049$

Application Example

6. How many small cubes are in the stack?

$$3^3 = 3 \cdot 3 \cdot 3$$
$$= 27$$

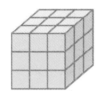

27 small cubes are in the stack.

PRACTICE MAKES PURR-FECT™

Check your answers at BigIdeasMath.com.

Find the value.

7. $3^4 =$ _____

8. $4^5 =$ _____

9. $12^3 =$ _____

10. $18^1 =$ _____

11. $5^6 =$ _____

12. $2^{10} =$ _____

13. $8^2 =$ _____

14. $7^3 =$ _____

Use an exponent to rewrite the expression.

15. $4 \cdot 4 \cdot 4 \cdot 4 =$ _____

16. $1 \cdot 1 \cdot 1 =$ _____

17. $5 \cdot 5 \cdot 5 =$ _____

18. $3 \cdot 3 \cdot 3 \cdot 3 \cdot 3 =$ _____

How many small cubes are in the stack?

19.  _____

_____

_____

20. 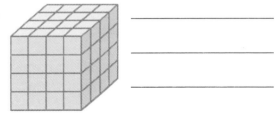 _____

_____

21. **FLYING SAUCERS** You saw 5 flying saucers. Each flying saucer had 5 aliens. Each alien had 5 eyes. How many alien eyes were there altogether? Explain your reasoning.

_____

REVIEW: Order of Operations

Name _____

Key Concept and Vocabulary

"**P**lease **E**xcuse **M**y **D**ear **A**unt **S**ally"

1st **P**arentheses

2nd **E**xponents

3rd **M**ultiplication and **D**ivision (from left to right)

4th **A**ddition and **S**ubtraction (from left to right)

Simplify $4^2 \div 2 + 3(9 - 5)$.

$$4^2 \div 2 + 3(9 - 5) = 4^2 \div 2 + 3 \cdot 4$$
$$= 16 \div 2 + 3 \cdot 4$$
$$= 8 + 12$$
$$= 20$$

Order of Operations

Skill Examples

1. $18 \div 2 - 4 = 9 - 4 = 5$

2. $12 \cdot (6 - 2) = 12 \cdot 4 = 48$

3. $14 \cdot 3 - 19 = 42 - 19 = 23$

4. $20 \div 10 + 21 \cdot 5 = 2 + 105 = 107$

5. $(2 + 3)^2 - 5 = 25 - 5 = 20$

Application Example

6. At a museum, 4 adults pay $5 each and 6 children pay $3 each. What is the total cost of the tickets?

$$4 \cdot 5 + 6 \cdot 3 = 20 + 18$$
$$= 38$$

The total cost is $38.

PRACTICE MAKES PURR-FECT™

Check your answers at BigIdeasMath.com.

Simplify.

7. $3^2 + 5(4 - 2) =$ _____

8. $3 + 4 \div 2 =$ _____

9. $10 \div 5 \cdot 3 =$ _____

10. $4(3^3 - 8) \div 2 =$ _____

11. $3 \cdot 6 - 4 \div 2 =$ _____

12. $12 + 7 \cdot 3 - 24 =$ _____

Insert parentheses to make the statement true.

13. $5^2 - 15 \div 5 = 2$

14. $12 \cdot 2^3 + 4 = 144$

15. $91 - 21 \div 7 = 10$

Write an expression for the total area of the two rectangles. Evaluate your expression.

16.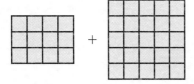

17.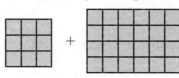

_____

_____

18. **ADMISSION** At a baseball game, 6 adults pay $20 each and 4 children pay $10 each. What is the total cost of the tickets? _____

19. **INSERTING PARENTHESES** Insert parentheses in the expression $4 + 2^3 - 5 \cdot 2$ in two ways: (a) so that the value is 10 and (b) so that the value is 14.

    (a) _____

    (b) _____

REVIEW: Cubes

Name _____

Key Concept and Vocabulary

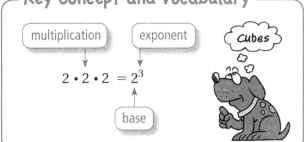

multiplication   exponent   Cubes

$$2 \cdot 2 \cdot 2 = 2^3$$

base

Visual Model

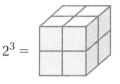

$2^3 =$

Skill Examples

1. $2^3 = 2 \cdot 2 \cdot 2 = 8$

2. $5^3 = 5 \cdot 5 \cdot 5 = 125$

3. $7^3 = 7 \cdot 7 \cdot 7 = 343$

4. $9^3 = 9 \cdot 9 \cdot 9 = 729$

5. $20^3 = 20 \cdot 20 \cdot 20 = 8000$

Application Example

6. How many small cubes are in the stack?

$$4^3 = 4 \cdot 4 \cdot 4$$
$$= 64$$

64 small cubes are in the stack.

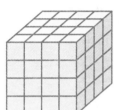

PRACTICE MAKES PURR-FECT™

Check your answers at BigIdeasMath.com.

Find the value.

7. $6^3 =$ _____

8. $3^3 =$ _____

9. $8^3 =$ _____

10. $10^3 =$ _____

11. $12^3 =$ _____

12. $15^3 =$ _____

Use an exponent to rewrite the expression.

13. $16 \cdot 16 \cdot 16 =$ _____

14. $11 \cdot 11 \cdot 11 =$ _____

15. $25 \cdot 25 \cdot 25 =$ _____

Evaluate the expression when $x = 3$.

16. $x^3 + 1$ _____

17. $2x^3$ _____

18. $6x - x^3$ _____

How many small cubes are in the stack?

19. 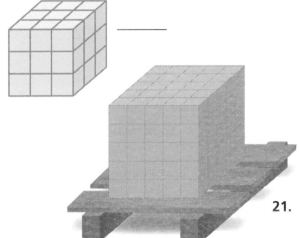 _____

20. 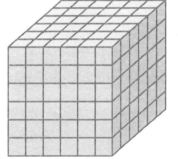 _____

21. **SHIPPING** How many boxes are on the pallet?

_____

REVIEW: Comparing, Ordering, and Graphing Integers

Name _____

Key Concept and Vocabulary

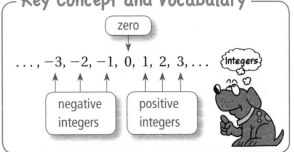

zero

..., −3, −2, −1, 0, 1, 2, 3, ... Integers

negative integers   positive integers

Visual Model

Number Line

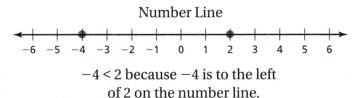

−4 < 2 because −4 is to the left of 2 on the number line.

Skill Examples

1. $0 \le 4$ "0 is less than or equal to 4"

2. $-1 > -3$ "−1 is greater than −3"

3. $-2 < -1$ "−2 is less than −1"

4. $2 > -2$ "2 is greater than −2"

5. $3 \ge 2$ "3 is greater than or equal to 2"

Application Example

6. The temperature in Seattle is 4°F. The temperature in Denver is −6°F. Which temperature is greater?

    $-6 < 4$ "−6 is less than 4"

    The temperature is greater in Seattle.

PRACTICE MAKES PURR-FECT™

Check your answers at BigIdeasMath.com.

Graph the two numbers. Then compare them using < or >.

7. $-3 \;\square\; 2$

8. $-1 \;\square\; 0$

9. $-1 \;\square\; -4$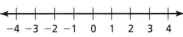

10. $1 \;\square\; 3$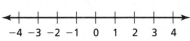

11. $0 \;\square\; 2$

12. $3 \;\square\; -1$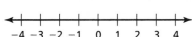

Order the temperatures from least to greatest.

13. −5°F, 13°F, 0°F, 5°F, 2°F, 20°F

    _____

14. 7°C, −4°C, −11°C, 0°C, 8°C, −12°C

    _____

Use an integer to describe the real-life situation.

15. A *profit* of $5 _____

    A *loss* of $5 _____

16. A *depth* of 8 ft _____

    A *height* of 4 ft _____

17. A *decrease* of 5°F _____

    An *increase* of 8°F _____

18. **BUSINESS LOSS** During its first week, a business had a loss that was greater than $4, but less than $6. Circle each integer that could represent this loss.

    −$7, −$6, −$5, −$4, −$3, −$2, −$1, $0, $1, $2, $3, $4, $5, $6, $7

REVIEW: Coordinate Plane

Name _____

Key Concept and Vocabulary

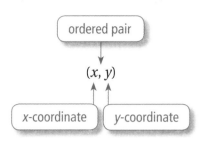

ordered pair

(x, y)

x-coordinate   y-coordinate

Skill Examples

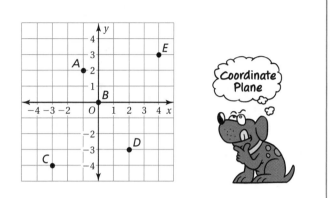

1. $A(-1, 2)$ (Quadrant II)
2. $B(0, 0)$ (origin)
3. $C(-3, -4)$ (Quadrant III)
4. $D(2, -3)$ (Quadrant IV)
5. $E(4, 3)$ (Quadrant I)

PRACTICE MAKES PURR-FECT™

Check your answers at BigIdeasMath.com.

Write the ordered pair that represents the point in the coordinate plane.

6. F _____

7. G _____

8. H _____

9. I _____

10. J _____

Plot the ordered pair in the coordinate plane. Name the quadrant for the point.

11. $K(-3, 5)$ _____

12. $L(-3, 0)$ _____

13. $M(2, 5)$ _____

14. $N(4, -2)$ _____

15. $P(-2, -4)$ _____

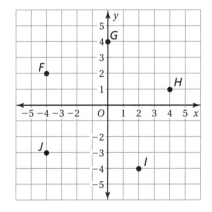

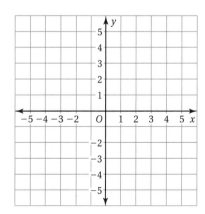

REVIEW: Adding and Subtracting Integers

Name _____

Key Concept and Vocabulary

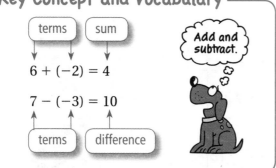

terms   sum

$6 + (-2) = 4$

$7 - (-3) = 10$

terms   difference

Add and subtract.

Visual Model

To add a positive number, move to the *right*.

$$-5 + 8 = 3$$

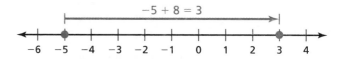

To subtract a positive number, move to the *left*.

Skill Examples

1. $5 + (-3) = 5 - 3 = 2$
2. $5 - (-2) = 5 + 2 = 7$
3. $-2 + 4 = 2$
4. $-3 - (-2) = -3 + 2 = -1$
5. $8 - (-3) = 8 + 3 = 11$

To subtract, change the sign and add.

Application Example

6. The temperature is 8°F in the morning and drops to −5°F in the evening. What is the difference between these temperatures?

$$8 - (-5) = 8 + 5$$
$$= 13$$

The difference is 13 degrees.

PRACTICE MAKES *PURR*-FECT™

Check your answers at BigIdeasMath.com.

Find the sum or difference.

7. $-2 + 3 =$ ____
8. $-4 - 5 =$ ____
9. $8 - 2 =$ ____
10. $8 - (-2) =$ ____

11. $-4 - (-1) =$ ____
12. $-5 + (-5) =$ ____
13. $4 - (-8) =$ ____
14. $4 - 8 =$ ____

15. $-4 + (-6) =$ ____
16. $-4 - (-6) =$ ____
17. $10 - 13 =$ ____
18. $13 - (-10) =$ ____

Write the addition or subtraction shown by the number line.

19.
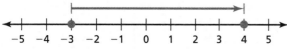

20.
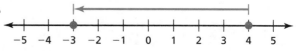

21. **TEMPERATURE** The temperature is 16°F in the morning and drops to −15°F in the evening. What is the difference between these temperatures? _____

22. **SUBMARINE** A submarine is 450 feet below sea level. It descends 300 feet. What is its new position? Show your work.

_____

_____

REVIEW: Multiplying and Dividing Integers

Name _____

Key Concept and Vocabulary

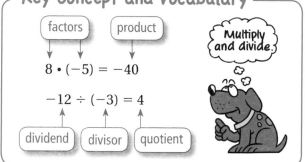

factors   product

$8 \cdot (-5) = -40$

$-12 \div (-3) = 4$

dividend   divisor   quotient

Multiply and divide.

Visual Model

$$4 \cdot (-2) = (-2) + (-2) + (-2) + (-2)$$

Skill Examples

1. $-3 \cdot (-4) = 12$ ← same sign, product and quotient positive

2. $-36 \div (-6) = 6$ ←

3. $-7 \cdot 0 = 0$

4. $-10 \div 5 = -2$ ← different signs, product and quotient negative

5. $-5 \cdot 6 = -30$ ←

Application Example

6. Each of your six friends owes you $5. Use integer multiplication to represent the total amount your friends owe you.

$$6 \cdot (-5) = -30$$

∴ The total amount owed is $30.

PRACTICE MAKES *PURR*-FECT™

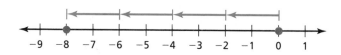

Check your answers at BigIdeasMath.com.

Find the product or quotient.

7. $-3 \times (-5) =$ _____   **8.** $7(-3) =$ _____   **9.** $0 \cdot (-5) =$ _____   **10.** $(-5)(-7) =$ _____

11. $-8 \cdot 2 =$ _____   **12.** $(-5)^2 =$ _____   **13.** $(-3)^3 =$ _____   **14.** $4(-2)(-3) =$ _____

15. $-16 \div 4 =$ _____   **16.** $-20 \div (-5) =$ _____   **17.** $\dfrac{-9}{3} =$ _____   **18.** $\dfrac{-20}{-10} =$ _____

Complete the multiplication or division equation.

19. $-15 \div$ _____ $= -3$ **20.** $45 \div$ _____ $= -5$ **21.** _____ $\div (-20) = 5$

22. $8 \cdot$ _____ $= -64$ **23.** _____ $\cdot (-9) = 27$ **24.** $-12 \cdot$ _____ $= -96$

25. **TOTAL OWED** Each of your eight friends owes you $10. Use integer multiplication to represent the total amount your friends owe you. _____

_____

26. **TEMPERATURE** The low temperatures for a week in Edmonton, Alberta are $-15°C$, $-12°C$, $-10°C$, $-12°C$, $-18°C$, $-20°C$, and $-25°C$. What is the mean low temperature for the week? Show your work.

_____

_____

REVIEW: Equivalent Fractions

Name _____

$$\frac{2}{3} = \frac{2 \cdot 4}{3 \cdot 4} = \frac{8}{12}$$

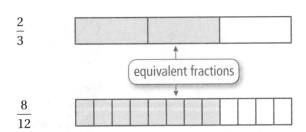

Equivalent Fractions

Multiply numerator and denominator by the same number.

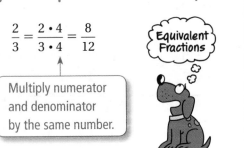

Visual Model

$\frac{2}{3}$

equivalent fractions

$\frac{8}{12}$

Skill Examples

1. $\frac{1}{2} = \frac{1 \cdot 2}{2 \cdot 2} = \frac{2}{4}$

   $\frac{1}{2}, \frac{2}{4},$ and $\frac{3}{6}$ are all equivalent.

2. $\frac{1}{2} = \frac{1 \cdot 3}{2 \cdot 3} = \frac{3}{6}$

3. $\frac{3}{4} = \frac{3 \cdot 5}{4 \cdot 5} = \frac{15}{20}$

4. $\frac{4}{5} = \frac{4 \cdot 20}{5 \cdot 20} = \frac{80}{100}$

Application Example

5. You eat two-thirds of a pizza that has 12 pieces. How many pieces do you eat?

   $$\frac{2}{3} = \frac{2 \cdot 4}{3 \cdot 4} = \frac{8}{12}$$

   You eat 8 pieces.

PRACTICE MAKES PURR-FECT™

Check your answers at BigIdeasMath.com.

Write a fraction that is equivalent to the given fraction.

6. $\frac{1}{2} = \frac{\square}{4}$

7. $\frac{3}{5} = \frac{\square}{15}$

8. $\frac{4}{3} = \frac{\square}{9}$

9. $\frac{1}{3} = \frac{\square}{27}$

10. $\frac{2}{5} = \frac{\square}{20}$

11. $\frac{7}{8} = \frac{\square}{64}$

12. $\frac{3}{7} = \frac{6}{\square}$

13. $\frac{9}{4} = \frac{36}{\square}$

14. $\frac{1}{5} = \frac{10}{\square}$

15. $\frac{3}{9} = \frac{12}{\square}$

16. $\frac{7}{10} = \frac{14}{\square}$

17. $\frac{3}{8} = \frac{9}{\square}$

Shade the model so that the fraction is equivalent.

18. 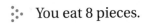 =

19. =

20. **PIZZA** You eat three-fourths of a pizza that has 12 pieces. How many pieces do you eat? _____

21. **SURVEY** A survey asked 240 people if they liked the movie "Star Wars." One-third liked it, one-sixth did not like it, and one-half had not seen it. How many people are in each of the three categories? _____

REVIEW: Simplifying Fractions

Name _____

Key Concept and Vocabulary

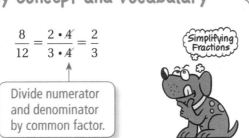

$$\frac{8}{12} = \frac{2 \cdot 4}{3 \cdot 4} = \frac{2}{3}$$

Divide numerator and denominator by common factor.

Simplifying Fractions

Visual Model

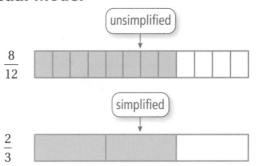

unsimplified

$\frac{8}{12}$

simplified

$\frac{2}{3}$

Skill Examples

1. $\dfrac{2}{4} = \dfrac{1 \cdot 2}{2 \cdot 2} = \dfrac{1}{2}$

2. $\dfrac{3}{6} = \dfrac{1 \cdot 3}{2 \cdot 3} = \dfrac{1}{2}$

3. $\dfrac{15}{20} = \dfrac{3 \cdot 5}{4 \cdot 5} = \dfrac{3}{4}$

4. $\dfrac{80}{100} = \dfrac{4 \cdot 20}{5 \cdot 20} = \dfrac{4}{5}$

Application Example

5. Five of the 25 students in your class have a Facebook account. Write this fraction in simplifed form.

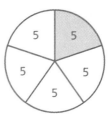

$$\frac{5}{25} = \frac{1 \cdot 5}{5 \cdot 5} = \frac{1}{5}$$

One-fifth of your class has a Facebook account.

PRACTICE MAKES PURR-FECT™

Check your answers at BigIdeasMath.com.

Simplify the fraction.

6. $\dfrac{16}{18} =$ _____

7. $\dfrac{10}{12} =$ _____

8. $\dfrac{6}{8} =$ _____

9. $\dfrac{15}{45} =$ _____

10. $\dfrac{12}{40} =$ _____

11. $\dfrac{14}{21} =$ _____

12. $\dfrac{6}{2} =$ _____

13. $\dfrac{20}{50} =$ _____

14. $\dfrac{12}{30} =$ _____

15. $\dfrac{20}{15} =$ _____

16. $\dfrac{75}{85} =$ _____

17. $\dfrac{21}{35} =$ _____

Shade the model so that the fraction is simplified.

18.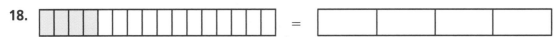

19.

20. **FACEBOOK** Eight of the 24 students in your class have a Facebook account. Write this fraction in simplified form. _____

21. **SIMPLIFYING** Write five different fractions that each simplify to two-fifths.

_____

REVIEW: Estimating Fraction Sums and Differences

Name _____

Key Concept and Vocabulary

$$\frac{7}{8} + \frac{1}{6} \approx 1 + 0 = 1$$

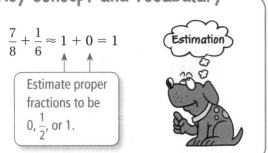

Estimate proper fractions to be $0, \frac{1}{2},$ or 1.

Estimation

Visual Model

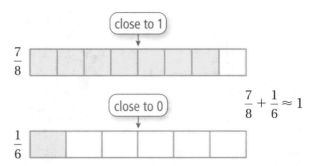

close to 1

$\frac{7}{8}$

close to 0

$\frac{1}{6}$

$$\frac{7}{8} + \frac{1}{6} \approx 1$$

Skill Examples

1. $\dfrac{3}{7} + \dfrac{3}{8} \approx \dfrac{1}{2} + \dfrac{1}{2} = 1$

2. $\dfrac{8}{9} - \dfrac{5}{8} \approx 1 - \dfrac{1}{2} = \dfrac{1}{2}$

3. $\dfrac{9}{10} + \dfrac{6}{7} \approx 1 + 1 = 2$

4. $\dfrac{5}{12} - \dfrac{1}{16} \approx \dfrac{1}{2} - 0 = \dfrac{1}{2}$

Application Example

5. Approximate the width of the window.

$$6\frac{5}{8} + 5\frac{7}{8} \approx 6\frac{1}{2} + 6$$
$$= 12\frac{1}{2}$$

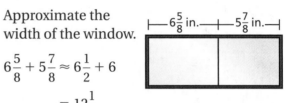

$\longmapsto 6\frac{5}{8}$ in.$\longmapsto 5\frac{7}{8}$ in.$\longmapsto$

⋮ The window is about $12\frac{1}{2}$ inches wide.

PRACTICE MAKES PURR-FECT™

Check your answers at BigIdeasMath.com.

Estimate the sum or difference.

6. $\dfrac{5}{9} + \dfrac{3}{7} \approx$ _____

7. $\dfrac{6}{11} + \dfrac{11}{13} \approx$ _____

8. $\dfrac{1}{10} + \dfrac{15}{8} \approx$ _____

9. $\dfrac{11}{9} + \dfrac{6}{7} \approx$ _____

10. $\dfrac{9}{10} - \dfrac{5}{11} \approx$ _____

11. $\dfrac{17}{8} - \dfrac{3}{5} \approx$ _____

12. $\dfrac{11}{9} - \dfrac{1}{8} \approx$ _____

13. $\dfrac{5}{2} - \dfrac{3}{7} \approx$ _____

14. $1\dfrac{4}{5} + 2\dfrac{1}{7} \approx$ _____

15. $2\dfrac{4}{7} + 3\dfrac{3}{5} \approx$ _____

16. $5\dfrac{9}{10} - 4\dfrac{6}{10} \approx$ _____

17. $1\dfrac{4}{5} - \dfrac{11}{14} \approx$ _____

Approximate the width of the window.

18.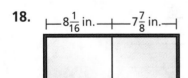

$\longmapsto 8\frac{1}{16}$ in.$\longmapsto 7\frac{7}{8}$ in.$\longmapsto$

_____

19. $\longmapsto 24\frac{9}{10}$ cm$\longmapsto 25\frac{1}{10}$ cm$\longmapsto$

_____

20. **DISTANCE** You walked $2\dfrac{1}{5}$ miles on Monday and $3\dfrac{7}{8}$ miles on Tuesday. Estimate the total number of miles you walked on Monday and Tuesday. _____

21. **ESTIMATION STRATEGY** Estimating a fraction to be $0, \dfrac{1}{2},$ or 1 does not work well with fractions such as $\dfrac{1}{4}$ and $\dfrac{3}{4}$. Why?

REVIEW: Comparing and Ordering Fractions

Name _____

Key Concept and Vocabulary

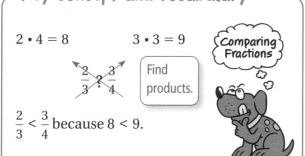

$2 \cdot 4 = 8$ $3 \cdot 3 = 9$

$\dfrac{2}{3} \cdot \dfrac{3}{4}$ Find products.   Comparing Fractions

$\dfrac{2}{3} < \dfrac{3}{4}$ because $8 < 9$.

Visual Model

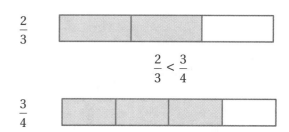

$\dfrac{2}{3}$

$\dfrac{2}{3} < \dfrac{3}{4}$

$\dfrac{3}{4}$

Skill Examples

1. $\dfrac{1}{2} > \dfrac{5}{11}$ because $1 \cdot 11 > 2 \cdot 5.$

2. $\dfrac{3}{6} = \dfrac{1}{2}$ because $3 \cdot 2 = 6 \cdot 1.$

3. $\dfrac{3}{8} < \dfrac{2}{5}$ because $3 \cdot 5 < 8 \cdot 2.$

4. $\dfrac{4}{9} > \dfrac{3}{7}$ because $4 \cdot 7 > 9 \cdot 3.$

Application Example

5. You run seven-eighths mile. Your friend runs eight-tenths mile. Who runs farther?

   $\dfrac{7}{8} > \dfrac{8}{10}$ because $7 \cdot 10 > 8 \cdot 8.$

   ⋮⋮ You run farther.

PRACTICE MAKES *PURR*-FECT™

Check your answers at BigIdeasMath.com.

Compare the fractions using <, >, or =.

6. $\dfrac{4}{5} \boxed{} \dfrac{8}{11}$

7. $\dfrac{6}{7} \boxed{} \dfrac{5}{6}$

8. $\dfrac{6}{7} \boxed{} \dfrac{7}{8}$

9. $\dfrac{3}{11} \boxed{} \dfrac{6}{22}$

10. $\dfrac{9}{2} \boxed{} \dfrac{14}{3}$

11. $\dfrac{3}{9} \boxed{} \dfrac{1}{3}$

12. $\dfrac{4}{9} \boxed{} \dfrac{9}{20}$

13. $\dfrac{7}{12} \boxed{} \dfrac{4}{7}$

14. $\dfrac{2}{9} \boxed{} \dfrac{4}{18}$

15. $\dfrac{3}{8} \boxed{} \dfrac{4}{11}$

16. $\dfrac{7}{5} \boxed{} \dfrac{13}{9}$

17. $\dfrac{6}{5} \boxed{} \dfrac{11}{10}$

Compare the fractions models using <, >, or =.

18.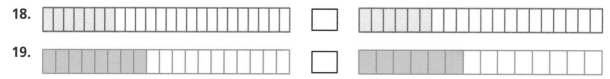

19.

20. **MILK** You drink six-eighths of a quart of milk. Your friend pours a quart of milk into four 8-fluid ounce glasses and drinks three of them. Who drinks more? _____

21. **ORDERING FRACTIONS** Order the fractions from least to greatest and graph them on a number line: $\dfrac{3}{8}, \dfrac{1}{4}, \dfrac{1}{3},$ and $\dfrac{2}{5}$.

Skills Review Topic 5.4

REVIEW: Adding and Subtracting Fractions with Like Denominators

Name _____

Key Concept and Vocabulary

$$\frac{2}{5} + \frac{1}{5} = \frac{2+1}{5} = \frac{3}{5}$$

Like Denominators

Add or subtract numerators.

$$\frac{2}{5} - \frac{1}{5} = \frac{2-1}{5} = \frac{1}{5}$$

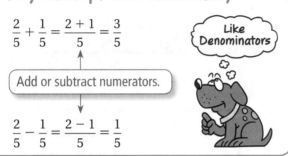

Visual Model

$\frac{2}{5}$

$+$ $\frac{1}{5}$

$\frac{3}{5}$

Skill Examples

1. $\frac{3}{8} + \frac{3}{8} = \frac{3+3}{8} = \frac{6}{8} = \frac{3}{4}$

2. $\frac{3}{4} + \frac{1}{4} = \frac{3+1}{4} = \frac{4}{4} = 1$

3. $\frac{7}{10} - \frac{4}{10} = \frac{7-4}{10} = \frac{3}{10}$

4. $\frac{13}{25} - \frac{8}{25} = \frac{13-8}{25} = \frac{5}{25} = \frac{1}{5}$

Application Example

5. On Monday, you painted two-fifths of a house. On Tuesday, you painted the same amount. How much is left?

$$\frac{5}{5} - \left(\frac{2}{5} + \frac{2}{5}\right) = \frac{5}{5} - \frac{4}{5} = \frac{1}{5}$$

⋰ You have one-fifth left to paint.

PRACTICE MAKES PURR-FECT™

Check your answers at BigIdeasMath.com.

Find the sum or difference. Write your answer in simplified form.

6. $\frac{1}{9} + \frac{2}{9} =$ _____

7. $\frac{6}{11} + \frac{5}{11} =$ _____

8. $\frac{1}{10} + \frac{3}{10} =$ _____

9. $\frac{3}{4} + \frac{2}{4} =$ _____

10. $\frac{3}{8} + \frac{1}{8} =$ _____

11. $\frac{1}{5} + \frac{2}{5} + \frac{2}{5} =$ _____

12. $\frac{5}{8} - \frac{1}{8} =$ _____

13. $\frac{6}{7} - \frac{3}{7} =$ _____

14. $\frac{7}{9} - \frac{4}{9} =$ _____

15. $\frac{9}{10} - \frac{7}{10} =$ _____

16. $\frac{5}{6} - \frac{2}{6} =$ _____

17. $\frac{6}{6} - \left(\frac{1}{6} + \frac{2}{6}\right) =$ _____

Find the perimeter of the rectangle or triangle.

18. $\frac{1}{4}$ ft, $\frac{2}{4}$ ft

Perimeter = _____

19. $\frac{2}{5}$ cm, $\frac{3}{5}$ cm

Perimeter = _____

20. 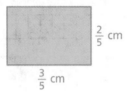 $\frac{3}{8}$ in. $\frac{3}{8}$ in. $\frac{4}{8}$ in.

Perimeter = _____

21. 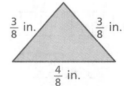 $\frac{4}{10}$ m $\frac{2}{10}$ m $\frac{3}{10}$ m

Perimeter = _____

22. **REACHING YOUR GOAL** You have a savings goal. In January, you saved $\frac{2}{10}$ of your goal.

In February, you saved $\frac{3}{10}$ more. How much of your goal remains? Explain.

REVIEW: Adding and Subtracting Fractions with Unlike Denominators

Name _____

Key Concept and Vocabulary

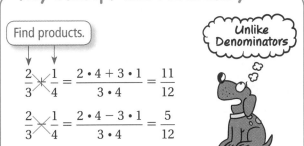

Find products.

$$\frac{2}{3} \times \frac{1}{4} = \frac{2 \cdot 4 + 3 \cdot 1}{3 \cdot 4} = \frac{11}{12}$$

$$\frac{2}{3} \times \frac{1}{4} = \frac{2 \cdot 4 - 3 \cdot 1}{3 \cdot 4} = \frac{5}{12}$$

Unlike Denominators

Visual Model

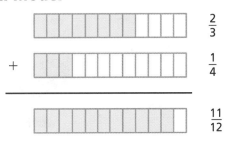

$\frac{2}{3}$

$+$ $\frac{1}{4}$

$\frac{11}{12}$

Skill Examples

1. $\dfrac{1}{5} + \dfrac{2}{3} = \dfrac{1 \cdot 3 + 5 \cdot 2}{5 \cdot 3} = \dfrac{13}{15}$

2. $\dfrac{1}{2} + \dfrac{1}{4} = \dfrac{1 \cdot 4 + 2 \cdot 1}{2 \cdot 4} = \dfrac{6}{8} = \dfrac{3}{4}$

3. $\dfrac{1}{3} - \dfrac{1}{4} = \dfrac{1 \cdot 4 - 3 \cdot 1}{3 \cdot 4} = \dfrac{1}{12}$

4. $\dfrac{3}{7} - \dfrac{2}{5} = \dfrac{3 \cdot 5 - 7 \cdot 2}{7 \cdot 5} = \dfrac{1}{35}$

Application Example

5. You ride your bike $\dfrac{3}{8}$ mile to the store. Then you ride $\dfrac{1}{6}$ mile to school. How far do you ride altogether?

$$\frac{3}{8} + \frac{1}{6} = \frac{3 \cdot 6 + 8 \cdot 1}{8 \cdot 6} = \frac{26}{48} = \frac{13}{24}$$

You ride $\dfrac{13}{24}$ mile.

PRACTICE MAKES *PURR-FECT*™

Check your answers at BigIdeasMath.com.

Find the sum or difference. Write your answer in simplified form.

6. $\dfrac{1}{3} + \dfrac{1}{8} =$ _____

7. $\dfrac{2}{3} + \dfrac{1}{5} =$ _____

8. $\dfrac{3}{10} + \dfrac{1}{4} =$ _____

9. $\dfrac{1}{2} + \dfrac{2}{5} =$ _____

10. $\dfrac{3}{7} + \dfrac{1}{3} =$ _____

11. $\dfrac{1}{8} + \dfrac{2}{5} =$ _____

12. $\dfrac{5}{8} - \dfrac{1}{3} =$ _____

13. $\dfrac{5}{6} - \dfrac{3}{5} =$ _____

14. $\dfrac{5}{9} - \dfrac{2}{5} =$ _____

15. $\dfrac{7}{10} - \dfrac{1}{4} =$ _____

16. $\dfrac{3}{5} - \dfrac{1}{6} =$ _____

17. $\dfrac{1}{5} - \dfrac{1}{6} =$ _____

Find the total distance from House A to House B and then to House C.

18.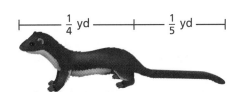

19.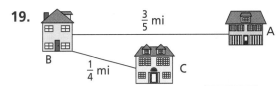

20. **WEASEL LENGTH** Find the total length of the weasel. _____

21. **IMPROVING YOUR SPEED** You swam at a rate of $\dfrac{3}{8}$ mile per hour in March. You swam at a rate of $\dfrac{3}{7}$ mile per hour in April. How much faster did you swim in April? _____

REVIEW: Multiplying Fractions

Name _____

Key Concept and Vocabulary

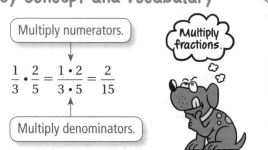

Multiply numerators.

$$\frac{1}{3} \cdot \frac{2}{5} = \frac{1 \cdot 2}{3 \cdot 5} = \frac{2}{15}$$

Multiply denominators.

Visual Model

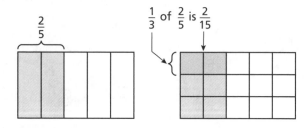

$\frac{1}{3}$ of $\frac{2}{5}$ is $\frac{2}{15}$

Skill Examples

1. $\frac{2}{3} \cdot \frac{1}{4} = \frac{2 \cdot 1}{3 \cdot 4} = \frac{2}{12} = \frac{1}{6}$

2. $\frac{3}{8} \times \frac{2}{9} = \frac{3 \cdot 2}{8 \cdot 9} = \frac{6}{72} = \frac{1}{12}$

3. $\left(\frac{2}{5}\right)\left(\frac{1}{4}\right) = \frac{2 \cdot 1}{5 \cdot 4} = \frac{2}{20} = \frac{1}{10}$

4. $\frac{1}{7} \cdot \frac{3}{5} = \frac{1 \cdot 3}{7 \cdot 5} = \frac{3}{35}$

Application Example

5. A recipe calls for three-fourths cup of flour. You want to make one-half of the recipe. How much flour should you use?

$$\frac{1}{2} \cdot \frac{3}{4} = \frac{1 \cdot 3}{2 \cdot 4} = \frac{3}{8}$$

⋯ You should use $\frac{3}{8}$ cup flour.

PRACTICE MAKES *PURR*-FECT™

Check your answers at BigIdeasMath.com.

Find the product. Write your answer in simplified form.

6. $\frac{1}{3} \cdot \frac{2}{7} =$ _____

7. $\frac{1}{2} \times \frac{1}{4} =$ _____

8. $\frac{1}{10} \cdot \frac{3}{10} =$ _____

9. $\frac{3}{2} \times \frac{2}{5} =$ _____

10. $\frac{3}{8} \times \frac{1}{2} =$ _____

11. $\left(\frac{1}{5}\right)\left(\frac{2}{5}\right) =$ _____

12. $\left(\frac{2}{3}\right)^2 =$ _____

13. $\frac{3}{2} \cdot \frac{2}{3} =$ _____

14. $\left(\frac{3}{1}\right)\left(\frac{1}{3}\right) =$ _____

15. $2 \cdot \frac{1}{4} =$ _____

16. $3 \times \frac{3}{4} =$ _____

17. $\frac{1}{3} \cdot \frac{3}{4} \cdot \frac{4}{5} =$ _____

Find the area of the rectangle or parallelogram.

18.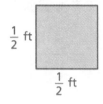

$\frac{1}{2}$ ft

$\frac{1}{2}$ ft

Area = _____

19.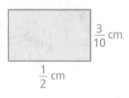

$\frac{3}{10}$ cm

$\frac{1}{2}$ cm

Area = _____

20.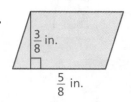

$\frac{3}{8}$ in.

$\frac{5}{8}$ in.

Area = _____

21.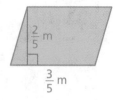

$\frac{2}{5}$ m

$\frac{3}{5}$ m

Area = _____

22. **OPEN-ENDED** Find three different pairs of fractions that have the same product.

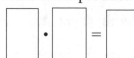

☐ · ☐ = ☐   ☐ · ☐ = ☐   ☐ · ☐ = ☐

REVIEW: Dividing Fractions

Name _____

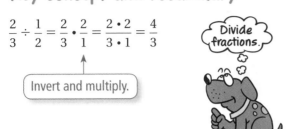

Visual Model

There are 2 "one-thirds" in two-thirds.

$$\frac{2}{3} \div \frac{1}{3} = \frac{2}{3} \cdot \frac{3}{1} = 2$$

$\frac{1}{3}$	$\frac{1}{3}$	

Skill Examples

1. $\dfrac{2}{5} \div \dfrac{1}{5} = \dfrac{2}{5} \cdot \dfrac{5}{1} = \dfrac{2 \cdot 5}{5 \cdot 1} = 2$

2. $\dfrac{2}{5} \div 5 = \dfrac{2}{5} \cdot \dfrac{1}{5} = \dfrac{2 \cdot 1}{5 \cdot 5} = \dfrac{2}{25}$

3. $\dfrac{9}{4} \div \dfrac{3}{4} = \dfrac{9}{4} \cdot \dfrac{4}{3} = \dfrac{9 \cdot 4}{4 \cdot 3} = 3$

4. $6 \div \dfrac{1}{2} = \dfrac{6}{1} \cdot \dfrac{2}{1} = \dfrac{6 \cdot 2}{1 \cdot 1} = 12$

Application Example

5. You drive 25 miles in one-half hour. What is your average rate?

$$25 \div \frac{1}{2} = \frac{25}{1} \cdot \frac{2}{1} = 50 \text{ mi/h} \qquad r = \frac{d}{t}$$

⋮⋗ Your average rate is 50 miles per hour.

PRACTICE MAKES PURR-FECT™

Check your answers at BigIdeasMath.com.

Find the quotient. Write your answer in simplified form.

6. $\dfrac{3}{5} \div \dfrac{1}{5} =$ _____

7. $4 \div \dfrac{1}{2} =$ _____

8. $\dfrac{2}{3} \div \dfrac{1}{6} =$ _____

9. $\dfrac{1}{6} \div \dfrac{2}{3} =$ _____

10. $\dfrac{2}{3} \div 2 =$ _____

11. $\dfrac{3}{4} \div 4 =$ _____

12. $\dfrac{3}{7} \div \dfrac{3}{7} =$ _____

13. $\dfrac{3}{7} \div \dfrac{7}{3} =$ _____

14. $5 \div \dfrac{1}{2} =$ _____

15. $\dfrac{9}{4} \div \dfrac{1}{4} =$ _____

16. $\dfrac{1}{4} \div \dfrac{1}{2} =$ _____

17. $\dfrac{3}{11} \div 11 =$ _____

Find the height of the rectangle or parallelogram.

18.
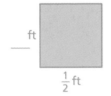
___ ft
$\frac{1}{2}$ ft
Area $= \dfrac{1}{4}$ ft^2

19.
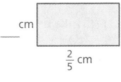
cm ___
$\frac{2}{5}$ cm
Area $= \dfrac{2}{25}$ cm^2

20.

in.
$\frac{3}{8}$ in.
Area $= \dfrac{3}{16}$ in.^{2}

21.
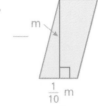
m
$\frac{1}{10}$ m
Area $= \dfrac{1}{50}$ m^2

22. **SPEED** You drive 15 miles in one-fourth hour. What is your average speed? _____

23. **MAGNETIC TAPE** A refrigerator magnet uses $\dfrac{5}{8}$ inch of magnetic tape. How many refrigerator magnets can you make with 10 inches of magnetic tape? Explain.

_____

REVIEW: Mixed Numbers and Improper Fractions

Name _____

Key Concept and Vocabulary

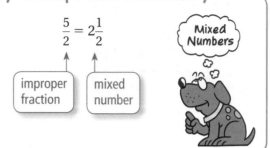

$$\frac{5}{2} = 2\frac{1}{2}$$

improper fraction   mixed number

Mixed Numbers

Visual Model

$$\frac{5}{2} \quad = \quad 2\frac{1}{2}$$

Skill Examples

1. $\frac{7}{3} = 2\frac{1}{3}$

2. $\frac{8}{4} = 2$

3. $2\frac{1}{4} = \frac{8}{4} + \frac{1}{4} = \frac{9}{4}$

4. $3\frac{3}{5} = \frac{15}{5} + \frac{3}{5} = \frac{18}{5}$

Application Example

5. During a month, you used 13 half-hours of phone time. How many hours did you use?

   13 halves $\rightarrow$ $\frac{13}{2} = 6\frac{1}{2}$ $\leftarrow$ 6 and one-half

   You used $6\frac{1}{2}$ hours.

PRACTICE MAKES PURR-FECT™

Check your answers at BigIdeasMath.com.

Write the improper fraction as a mixed number.

6. $\frac{4}{3} =$ _____

7. $\frac{3}{2} =$ _____

8. $\frac{8}{3} =$ _____

9. $\frac{9}{6} =$ _____

10. $\frac{7}{4} =$ _____

11. $\frac{28}{3} =$ _____

12. $\frac{19}{4} =$ _____

13. $\frac{11}{2} =$ _____

Write the mixed number as an improper fraction.

14. $2\frac{2}{3} =$ _____

15. $5\frac{1}{4} =$ _____

16. $3\frac{2}{5} =$ _____

17. $1\frac{3}{8} =$ _____

18. Rewrite the sentence using a mixed number. Susan drinks five-fourths of a quart of milk.

_____

19. Rewrite the sentence using an improper fraction. Tom runs for 2 and one quarter hours.

_____

20. **NUMBER LINE** Graph the improper fractions on the number line: $\frac{5}{3}, \frac{7}{2},$ and $\frac{13}{3}$.

REVIEW: Adding and Subtracting Mixed Numbers

Name _____

Key Concept and Vocabulary

$$2\frac{2}{3} + 1\frac{2}{3} = 3\frac{4}{3} = 4\frac{1}{3}$$

Add and subtract.

$$5\frac{1}{5} - 1\frac{3}{5} = 4\frac{6}{5} - 1\frac{3}{5} = 3\frac{3}{5}$$

Visual Model

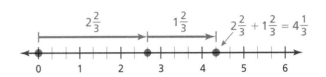

Skill Examples

1. $3\frac{1}{4} + 2\frac{1}{2} = 3\frac{1}{4} + 2\frac{2}{4} = 5\frac{3}{4}$

2. $5\frac{3}{5} + 1\frac{4}{5} = 6\frac{7}{5} = 7\frac{2}{5}$

3. $5\frac{5}{6} - 3\frac{1}{3} = 5\frac{5}{6} - 3\frac{2}{6} = 2\frac{3}{6} = 2\frac{1}{2}$

4. $4\frac{1}{3} - 1\frac{2}{3} = 3\frac{4}{3} - 1\frac{2}{3} = 2\frac{2}{3}$

Application Example

5. Find the perimeter of the triangle.

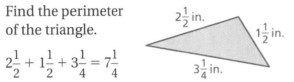

$$2\frac{1}{2} + 1\frac{1}{2} + 3\frac{1}{4} = 7\frac{1}{4}$$

The perimeter is $7\frac{1}{4}$ inches.

PRACTICE MAKES PURR-FECT™

Find the sum or difference. Write your answer in simplified form.

6. $4\frac{1}{4} + 2\frac{1}{4} =$ _____

7. $1\frac{2}{5} + 3\frac{1}{5} =$ _____

8. $5\frac{4}{5} + 3\frac{4}{5} =$ _____

9. $2\frac{2}{3} + 4\frac{1}{6} =$ _____

10. $7\frac{2}{3} + 3\frac{1}{3} =$ _____

11. $5\frac{1}{2} + 5\frac{1}{2} =$ _____

12. $3\frac{1}{4} - 2\frac{1}{2} =$ _____

13. $4\frac{3}{4} - 1\frac{1}{2} =$ _____

14. $8\frac{3}{5} - 5\frac{3}{5} =$ _____

15. $7\frac{1}{6} - 3\frac{1}{3} =$ _____

16. $1\frac{1}{4} - \frac{1}{2} =$ _____

17. $6\frac{3}{4} - 6\frac{1}{2} =$ _____

Find the perimeter of the triangle.

18.

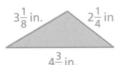

$3\frac{1}{8}$ in. $2\frac{1}{4}$ in.

$4\frac{3}{4}$ in.   Perimeter = _____

19.

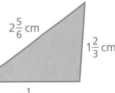

$2\frac{5}{6}$ cm $1\frac{2}{3}$ cm

$2\frac{1}{6}$ cm   Perimeter = _____

20. HEIGHT Sarah was $50\frac{1}{4}$ inches tall when she was 12 years old. She was $48\frac{1}{2}$ inches tall when she was 11 years old. How much did she grow during the year? _____

21. NUMBER LINE Show the sum graphically on the number line: $3\frac{1}{4} + 2\frac{1}{2}$.

REVIEW: Multiplying Mixed Numbers

Name _____

Key Concept and Vocabulary

$$2\frac{1}{2} \times 1\frac{1}{2} = \frac{5}{2} \times \frac{3}{2} = \frac{15}{4}$$

Multiply.

Rewrite as improper fractions.

Visual Model

$$\text{Area} = 2\frac{1}{2} \times 1\frac{1}{2} = \frac{15}{4} = 3\frac{3}{4}$$

Skill Examples

1. $3\frac{1}{2} \times 2\frac{1}{3} = \frac{7}{2} \times \frac{7}{3} = \frac{49}{6} = 8\frac{1}{6}$

2. $1\frac{3}{4} \cdot 4\frac{1}{2} = \frac{7}{4} \cdot \frac{9}{2} = \frac{63}{8} = 7\frac{7}{8}$

3. $2\frac{2}{5} \times 1\frac{2}{3} = \frac{12}{5} \times \frac{5}{3} = \frac{60}{15} = 4$

4. $\left(1\frac{1}{2}\right)\left(1\frac{1}{2}\right) = \left(\frac{3}{2}\right)\left(\frac{3}{2}\right) = \frac{9}{4} = 2\frac{1}{4}$

Application Example

5. Find the area of the triangle.

   $$\text{Area} = \frac{1}{2} \cdot 1\frac{1}{2} \cdot 3$$
   $$= \frac{1}{2} \cdot \frac{3}{2} \cdot \frac{3}{1} = \frac{9}{4} = 2\frac{1}{4}$$

   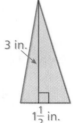
   3 in.
   $1\frac{1}{2}$ in.

   The area is $2\frac{1}{4}$ square inches.

PRACTICE MAKES PURR-FECT™

Find the product. Write your answer as a whole number or mixed number in simplified form.

6. $2\frac{1}{3} \times 1\frac{1}{3} =$ _____

7. $4\frac{2}{3} \times 1\frac{1}{2} =$ _____

8. $1\frac{1}{2} \times 3 =$ _____

9. $5\frac{1}{6} \times \frac{1}{3} =$ _____

10. $\frac{3}{4} \cdot 3\frac{1}{2} =$ _____

11. $5 \cdot 4\frac{1}{2} =$ _____

12. $2\frac{1}{7} \cdot \frac{7}{15} =$ _____

13. $1\frac{3}{5} \cdot \frac{3}{8} =$ _____

14. $\left(1\frac{1}{3}\right)^2 =$ _____

15. $\left(1\frac{1}{4}\right)^3 =$ _____

16. $\left(2\frac{1}{2}\right)\left(3\frac{1}{3}\right) =$ _____

17. $\left(3\frac{1}{2}\right)\left(\frac{1}{2}\right)^2 =$ _____

Find the area of the triangle.

18.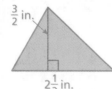
   $\frac{3}{2}$ in.
   $2\frac{1}{2}$ in.
   Area = _____

19.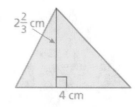
   $2\frac{2}{3}$ cm
   4 cm
   Area = _____

20. **RECIPE** Rewrite the recipe so that each item is one-third of the full recipe.

   $2\frac{1}{2}$ cups flour

   2 tsp baking powder

   4 Tbsp butter

   $\frac{1}{2}$ tsp salt

   $\frac{3}{4}$ cup milk

   _____ cups flour   _____ tsp salt

   _____ tsp baking powder   _____ cup milk

   _____ Tbsp butter

REVIEW: Dividing Mixed Numbers

Name _____

Key Concept and Vocabulary

Rewrite as improper fractions.

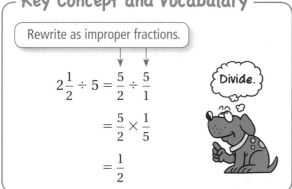

$$2\frac{1}{2} \div 5 = \frac{5}{2} \div \frac{5}{1}$$

$$= \frac{5}{2} \times \frac{1}{5}$$

$$= \frac{1}{2}$$

Divide.

Visual Model

Divide $2\frac{1}{2}$ into five equal parts. Each part is $\frac{1}{2}$.

$$2\frac{1}{2} \div 5 = \frac{1}{2}$$

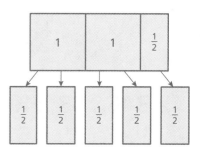

Skill Examples

1. $5 \div 2\frac{1}{2} = \frac{5}{1} \div \frac{5}{2} = \frac{5}{1} \times \frac{2}{5} = 2$

2. $3\frac{3}{4} \div 2\frac{1}{2} = \frac{15}{4} \div \frac{5}{2} = \frac{15}{4} \times \frac{2}{5} = \frac{3}{2} = 1\frac{1}{2}$

3. $4\frac{1}{6} \div 1\frac{2}{3} = \frac{25}{6} \div \frac{5}{3} = \frac{25}{6} \times \frac{3}{5} = \frac{5}{2} = 2\frac{1}{2}$

4. $7\frac{1}{3} \div 11 = \frac{22}{3} \div \frac{11}{1} = \frac{22}{3} \times \frac{1}{11} = \frac{2}{3}$

Application Example

5. You need $2\frac{1}{2}$ inches of ribbon to make a Blue-Ribbon award. How many awards can you make with 35 inches of ribbon?

$$35 \div 2\frac{1}{2} = \frac{35}{1} \div \frac{5}{2} = \frac{35}{1} \times \frac{2}{5} = 14$$

∴ You can make 14 awards.

PRACTICE MAKES *PURR-FECT*™

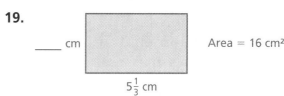

Check your answers at BigIdeasMath.com.

Find the quotient. Write your answer as a whole or mixed number in simplest form.

6. $4\frac{1}{2} \div 9 = $ _____

7. $3\frac{3}{7} \div 8 = $ _____

8. $4\frac{2}{3} \div 7 = $ _____

9. $1\frac{7}{9} \div 4 = $ _____

10. $8 \div 1\frac{1}{3} = $ _____

11. $32 \div 3\frac{1}{5} = $ _____

12. $11 \div 2\frac{3}{4} = $ _____

13. $9 \div 1\frac{1}{2} = $ _____

14. $5\frac{1}{2} \div \frac{1}{2} = $ _____

15. $\frac{1}{2} \div 1\frac{1}{2} = $ _____

16. $1\frac{1}{4} \div 1\frac{1}{4} = $ _____

17. $3\frac{1}{2} \div 1\frac{1}{3} = $ _____

Find the missing dimension.

18.

$2\frac{1}{2}$ ft

Area = 10 ft²

_____ ft

19.

_____ cm

Area = 16 cm²

$5\frac{1}{3}$ cm

20. **RED RIBBONS** You need $3\frac{1}{2}$ inches of ribbon to make a Red-Ribbon award. How many awards can you make with 35 inches of ribbon? _____

21. **SHIPPING** You are stacking books into a shipping box that is 15 inches high. Each book is $1\frac{1}{4}$ inches thick. How many books can you fit in a stack? _____

REVIEW: Decimal Place Value

Name _____

Key Concept and Vocabulary

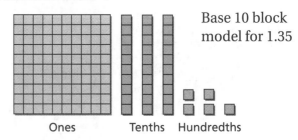

thousands
hundreds
tens
ones
tenths
hundredths
thousandths

2,346,783.3409

Visual Model

Ones   Tenths Hundredths

Base 10 block model for 1.35

Skill Examples

1. 156 = "One hundred fifty-six"

2. 1409 = "One thousand four hundred nine"

3. 14.009 = "Fourteen *and* nine thousandths"

4. 2.07 = "Two *and* seven hundredths"

Application Example

5. You are writing a check for $130.50. Write this amount in words.

One hundred thirty and 50/100.

PRACTICE MAKES *PURR*-FECT™

Check your answers at BigIdeasMath.com.

Write the number in words.

6. 27.35 = _____

7. 1560 = _____

Write the decimal number for the words.

8. "Five thousand seven hundred forty-nine *and* thirteen hundredths" = _____

9. "Nine hundred eighteen *and* fifty-seven thousandths" = _____

Write the decimal given by the model.

10.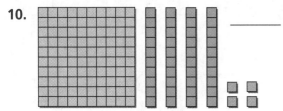

11.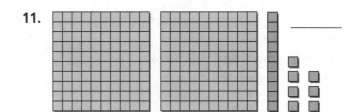

Write the words for the check.

12.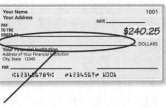

_____

13.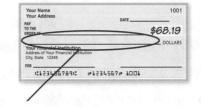

_____

REVIEW: Comparing and Ordering Decimals

Name _____

Key Concept and Vocabulary

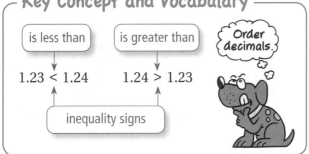

is less than → 1.23 < 1.24 ← inequality signs

is greater than → 1.24 > 1.23 ← inequality signs

Visual Model

Number Line

1.20 1.21 1.22 1.23 1.24 1.25 1.26

1.23 < 1.24 because 1.23 is to the left of 1.24 on the number line.

Skill Examples

1. 34.07 > 30.47

2. 12.35 < 12.351

3. 17,056.4 > 17,055.9

4. 0.004 < 0.030

5. 0.1003 > 0.0999

Application Example

6. Order the weights from least to greatest:
   12.3 lb, 11.9 lb, 12.0 lb, 13.1 lb.

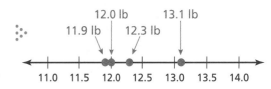

11.9 lb   12.0 lb   12.3 lb   13.1 lb

11.0 11.5 12.0 12.5 13.0 13.5 14.0

PRACTICE MAKES PURR-FECT™

Check your answers at BigIdeasMath.com.

Graph the two numbers. Then compare them using <, >, or =.

7. 1.6 ☐ 1.7

   0.8 1.0 1.2 1.4 1.6 1.8 2.0 2.2 2.4

8. 130.5 ☐ 103.5

   100   120   140   160

9. 9.2 ☐ 9.02

   9.0   9.1   9.2   9.3

10. 203.7 ☐ 207.3

    202   204   206   208   210

11. 0.32 ☐ 0.132

    0.0   0.1   0.2   0.3

12. 427.8 ☐ 428.3

    424   426   428   430

Order the lengths from least to greatest.

13. 32.5 ft, 29.9 ft, 32.3 ft, 31.7 ft, 31.75 ft

    _____

14. 0.5 mi, 0.05 mi, 0.47 mi, 1.02 mi, 0.08 mi

    _____

Is the scale balanced correctly?

15. _____
    1.22 lb   1.19 lb

16. _____
    18.03 oz   18.3 oz

17. _____
    0.05 kg   0.15 kg

18. **NUMBER LINE** On the number line, shade all values of x for which $x \le 3.2$ and $x \ge 2.9$.

    2.5 2.6 2.7 2.8 2.9 3.0 3.1 3.2 3.3 3.4 3.5 3.6

REVIEW: Fractions and Decimals

Name _____

Key Concept and Vocabulary

$\frac{1}{10} = 0.1$ $\frac{1}{5} = 0.2$ $\frac{2}{5} = 0.4$

$\frac{1}{4} = 0.25$ $\frac{1}{2} = 0.5$ $\frac{3}{4} = 0.75$

$\frac{1}{8} = 0.125$ $\frac{3}{8} = 0.375$ $\frac{5}{8} = 0.625$

Common Fractions

Visual Model

$\frac{1}{4} = 0.25$

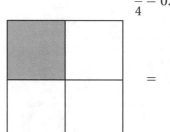

Skill Examples

1. $0.6 = \frac{6}{10} = \frac{3}{5}$

2. $\frac{4}{5} = \frac{4 \cdot 2}{5 \cdot 2} = \frac{8}{10} = 0.8$

3. $0.875 = \frac{875}{1000} = \frac{7 \cdot 125}{8 \cdot 125} = \frac{7}{8}$

4. $\frac{1}{3} = 0.333\ldots = 0.\overline{3}$ $\begin{array}{r} 0.3333\ldots \\ 3\overline{)1.0000\ldots} \end{array}$

Application Example

5. You put 16.75 gallons of gas in your car. Write this decimal as a mixed number.

$$16.75 = 16 + 0.75 = 16\frac{3}{4}$$

You put $16\frac{3}{4}$ gallons of gas in your car.

PRACTICE MAKES PURR-FECT™

Check your answers at BigIdeasMath.com.

Write the fraction as a decimal.

6. $\frac{3}{4} =$ _____

7. $\frac{7}{10} =$ _____

8. $\frac{3}{25} =$ _____

9. $\frac{7}{20} =$ _____

10. $\frac{19}{100} =$ _____

11. $\frac{11}{50} =$ _____

12. $\frac{2}{3} =$ _____

13. $\frac{1}{6} =$ _____

Write the decimal as a fraction.

14. $0.4 =$ _____

15. $0.35 =$ _____

16. $0.6 =$ _____

17. $1.5 =$ _____

Write the number represented by the model as a decimal and as a simplified fraction.

18. _____ = _____

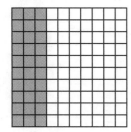

19. _____ = _____

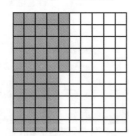

20. _____ = _____

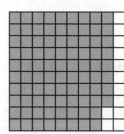

21. GAS You put 9.25 gallons of gas in your car. Write this decimal as a mixed number. _____

22. MULTIPLE FORMS Write the decimal 0.35 in two ways. One with a denominator of 100 and one with a denominator of 1000. _____

REVIEW: Rounding Decimals

Name _____

Key Concept and Vocabulary

Round up.

Decision digit is 5, 6, 7, 8, or 9.

Round down.

Decision digit is 0, 1, 2, 3, or 4.

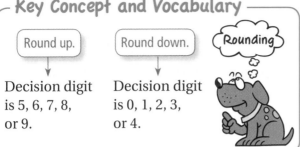

Rounding

Visual Model

Round to the *nearest tenth*.

3.63

3.63 rounds to 3.6 because 3.63 is closer to 3.6 than to 3.7.

Skill Examples

1. To the *nearest tenth*:
  4.78 rounds to 4.8.   Round up.

2. To the *nearest hundredth*:
  0.143 rounds to 0.14.   Round down.

3. To the *nearest thousandth*:
  0.0029 rounds to 0.003.   Round up.

Application Example

4. Gasoline costs $2.899 per gallon. Round this price to the nearest cent.

  To the *nearest cent*: 2.899 rounds to 2.90.

  ∴ The gasoline costs about $2.90 per gallon.

PRACTICE MAKES PURR-FECT™

Check your answers at BigIdeasMath.com.

Round to the nearest tenth. (The symbol ≈ means "is approximately to.")

5. 0.16 ≈ _____   **6.** 0.038 ≈ _____   **7.** 1.05 ≈ _____   **8.** 10.049 ≈ _____

Round to the nearest hundredth.

9. 0.0123 ≈ _____   **10.** 2.406 ≈ _____   **11.** 0.463 ≈ _____   **12.** 12.006 ≈ _____

Round to the nearest thousandth.

13. 0.0456 ≈ _____   **14.** 4.5062 ≈ _____   **15.** 1.0043 ≈ _____   **16.** 0.6666 ≈ _____

Round the butterfly's weight to the nearest hundredth of a gram.

17.   0.034 g

Weight ≈ _____

18.

0.107 g

Weight ≈ _____

19.

0.008 g

Weight ≈ _____

20. PRICE OF GAS Gasoline costs $2.379 per gallon. Round this price to the nearest cent. _____

21. BUTTERFLY WEIGHTS All species of butterflies weigh between 0.003 gram and 3 grams. Explain why it would not make sense to round some butterfly weights to the nearest hundredth of a gram.

_____

_____

REVIEW: Estimating Decimal Sums and Differences

Name _____

Key Concept and Vocabulary

$1.46 + 2.63 \approx 1.5 + 2.5 = 4$

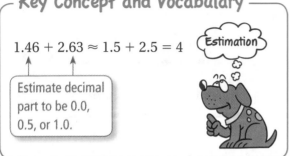

Estimation

Estimate decimal part to be 0.0, 0.5, or 1.0.

Visual Model

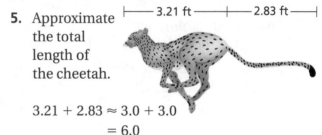

Close to 1

0.875

Close to 0

0.2

$0.875 + 0.2 \approx 1$

Skill Examples

1. $4.36 + 2.87 \approx 4.5 + 3.0 = 7.5$

2. $9.78 - 5.46 \approx 10.0 - 5.5 = 4.5$

3. $5.13 - 3.58 \approx 5.0 - 3.5 = 1.5$

4. $2.94 + 4.08 \approx 3.0 + 4.0 = 7.0$

Application Example

5. Approximate the total length of the cheetah.

|— 3.21 ft —|— 2.83 ft —|

$3.21 + 2.83 \approx 3.0 + 3.0$
$= 6.0$

The cheetah's total length is about 6 feet.

PRACTICE MAKES PURR-FECT™

Check your answers at BigIdeasMath.com.

Estimate the sum or difference.

6. $3.65 - 2.72 \approx$ _____

7. $9.03 - 6.78 \approx$ _____

8. $2.35 + 5.67 \approx$ _____

9. $8.21 - 4.11 \approx$ _____

10. $5.68 + 4.38 \approx$ _____

11. $3.92 + 3.92 \approx$ _____

12. $2.61 + 3.45 \approx$ _____

13. $2.07 - 1.45 \approx$ _____

14. $10.04 - 6.79 \approx$ _____

Approximate the total cost of the two shirts.

15. $17.89    $15.07

_____

16.  $23.49 $23.49

_____

17. **SHOPPING** At the grocery store, you buy items for $1.79, $3.15, $2.45, $9.08, and $3.49. Estimate the total amount you spend. _____

18. **MENTAL MATH** You buy 6 hamburgers that cost $3.45 each. Using only mental math, estimate the total amount of the 6 hamburgers.

_____

_____

REVIEW: Adding and Subtracting Decimals

Name _____

$$5.7$$
$$+ 3.36$$
$$\overline{9.06}$$

$$12.72$$
$$- 3.84$$
$$\overline{8.88}$$

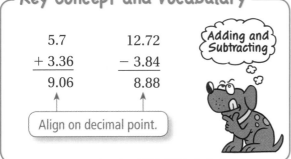

Adding and Subtracting

Align on decimal point.

Visual Model

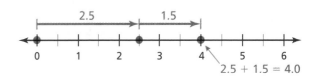

2.5 + 1.5 = 4.0

Skill Examples

1.
$$134.12$$
$$+ 25.485$$
$$\overline{159.605}$$

2.
$$0.135$$
$$+ 0.14$$
$$\overline{0.275}$$

3.
$$32.000$$
$$- 9.451$$
$$\overline{22.549}$$

4.
$$1.405$$
$$- 0.55$$
$$\overline{0.855}$$

Application Example

5. Find the perimeter of the triangle.

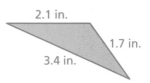

2.1 in.

1.7 in.

3.4 in.

$2.1 + 1.7 + 3.4 = 7.2$

The perimeter is 7.2 inches.

PRACTICE MAKES *PURR-FECT*™

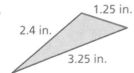

Check your answers at BigIdeasMath.com.

Find the sum or difference.

6. $4.75 + 3.56 =$ _____

7. $9.0 - 1.507 =$ _____

8. $2.4 + 2.04 =$ _____

9. $112.5 + 24.52 =$ _____

10. $5.7 - 4.81 =$ _____

11. $20 - 12.5 =$ _____

12. $2.3 + 3.4 + 5.9 =$ _____

13. $3.4 + 5.6 - 2.3 =$ _____

14. $10.0 - (4.5 + 2.3) =$ _____

Find the perimeter of the triangle.

15.

1.25 in.

2.4 in.

3.25 in.

Perimeter = _____

16.

2.4 cm

1.8 cm

3.7 cm

Perimeter = _____

17. **SHOPPING** You take $20 to the store. You buy a magazine for $3.65 and a birthday card for $5.29. How much money do you have left? _____

18. **NUMBER LINE** Show the sum graphically on the number line: $1.75 + 3.5$.

REVIEW: Multiplying Decimals

Name _____

Key Concept and Vocabulary

$$
\begin{array}{r}
2.1\,5 \quad\leftarrow \text{2 decimal places} \\
\times\,3.2 \quad\leftarrow +\text{ 1 decimal place} \\
\hline
4\,3\,0 \\
6\,4\,5 \\
\hline
6.8\,8\,0 \quad\leftarrow \text{3 decimal places}
\end{array}
$$

Multiply.

Visual Model

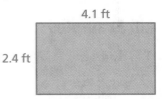

2.5

1.5

| 1 | 1 | 0.5 |
| 0.5 | 0.5 | 0.25 |

Area = $2.5 \times 1.5 = 3.75$

Skill Examples

1.
$$
\begin{array}{r}
4\,3.8 \\
\times\,1.5 \\
\hline
21\,9\,0 \\
4\,3\,8 \\
\hline
65.7\,0
\end{array}
$$

2.
$$
\begin{array}{r}
0.327 \\
\times\,24 \\
\hline
1\,308 \\
654 \\
\hline
7.848
\end{array}
$$

3.
$$
\begin{array}{r}
3\,2.5 \\
\times\,1.1\,3 \\
\hline
9\,7\,5 \\
3\,2\,5 \\
3\,2\,5 \\
\hline
3\,6.7\,2\,5
\end{array}
$$

Application Example

4. Find the area of the rectangle.

   $2.4 \times 4.1 = 9.84$

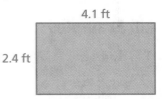

4.1 ft

2.4 ft

:: The area is 9.84 square feet.

PRACTICE MAKES PURR-FECT™

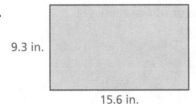

Check your answers at BigIdeasMath.com.

Find the product.

5. $3.02 \times 5.2 =$ _____

6. $1.75 \times 1 =$ _____

7. $(9.004)(0) =$ _____

8. $(4.05)^2 =$ _____

9. $2.25 \times 4 =$ _____

10. $(100.5)(90) =$ _____

11. $19.4 \times 5.05 =$ _____

12. $(1.2)(1.3)(1.4) =$ _____

13. $115 \times 3.2 =$ _____

14. $16(0.375) =$ _____

15. $(2.347)(1.8) =$ _____

16. $(1.5)^3 =$ _____

Find the area of the rectangle.

17.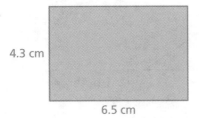

4.3 cm

6.5 cm

Area = _____

18.

9.3 in.

15.6 in.

Area = _____

19. **APPLES** Apples cost $3.45 per pound. Find the cost of 2.6 pounds of apples. _____

20. **PEACHES** Peaches cost $4.29 per pound. Find the cost of two and a quarter pounds of peaches. Show your work. _____

REVIEW: Dividing Decimals

Name _____

Key Concept and Vocabulary

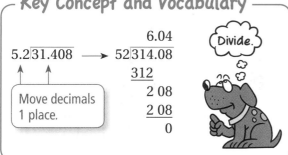

$$5.2\overline{)31.408} \longrightarrow 52\overline{)314.08}$$

6.04

312

2 08

2 08

0

Move decimals 1 place.

Divide.

Visual Model

$$12.5 \div 5 = 2.5$$

When you divide 12.5 into 5 equal parts, each part will be 2.5.

Skill Examples

1. $65.3 \div 10 = 6.53$

2. $65.3 \div 100 = 0.653$

3. $65.3 \div 1000 = 0.0653$

4. $65.3 \div 10{,}000 = 0.00653$

> Divide by a power of 10 by moving the decimal point.

Application Example

5. A prize of $104.32 is divided equally among four people. How much does each person get?

$$104.32 \div 4 = 26.08$$

Each person gets $26.08.

PRACTICE MAKES *PURR-FECT*™

Check your answers at BigIdeasMath.com.

Find the quotient.

6. $5.2 \div 10 =$ _____

7. $73.1 \div 100 =$ _____

8. $1500 \div 1000 =$ _____

9. $18.98 \div 3.65 =$ _____

10. $0.598 \div 2 =$ _____

11. $19.003 \div 1 =$ _____

12. $3.42 \div 0.36 =$ _____

13. $78.4 \div 1.4 =$ _____

14. $1000 \div 12.5 =$ _____

15. $0.45 \div 0.0125 =$ _____

16. $29.45 \div 4.75 =$ _____

17. $19.7 \div 0.1 =$ _____

Find the width of the rectangle.

18.

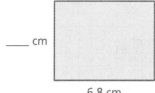

___ cm

Area = 35.36 cm^2

6.8 cm

19.

___ in.

15.2 in.

Area = 129.2 in.^{2}

20. **DRIVING TRIP** You drive 1400 miles in 3.5 days. What is the average number of miles you drive per day? _____

21. **METRIC SYSTEM** There are 2.54 centimeters in one inch. How many inches are there in 51.78 centimeters? Round your answer to the nearest tenth of an inch. _____

REVIEW: Percents

Name _____

Key Concept and Vocabulary

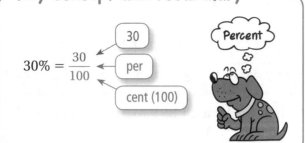

$30\% = \dfrac{30}{100}$

30 → per → cent (100)

Percent

Visual Model

30% is equal to 30 parts out of 100 parts.

Skill Examples

30% of 10 is 3:

$$\dfrac{30}{100} \cdot 10 = 3$$

1. 30% of 10 is 3: $\dfrac{30}{100} \cdot 10 = 3$

2. 25% of 8 is 2: $\dfrac{25}{100} \cdot 8 = 2$

3. 50% of 24 is 12: $\dfrac{50}{100} \cdot 24 = 12$

4. 75% of 80 is 60: $\dfrac{75}{100} \cdot 80 = 60$

Application Example

5. You earn $100,000 and have to pay 40% federal income tax. How much in federal income tax do you pay?

   40% of 100,000 is 40,000.

   ∴ You pay $40,000 in federal income tax.

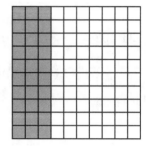

PRACTICE MAKES *PURR*-FECT™

Check your answers at BigIdeasMath.com.

Find the percent.

6. 20% of 50 = _____   7. 10% of 80 = _____   8. 1% of 100 = _____   9. 25% of 16 = _____

10. 30% of 40 = _____   11. 100% of 5 = _____   12. 60% of 60 = _____   13. 75% of 40 = _____

14. 25% of 200 = _____   15. 10% of 120 = _____   16. 0% of 10 = _____   17. 50% of 42 = _____

Shade the model to show the given percent.

18. 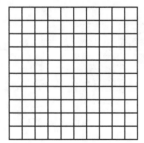 25% 19. 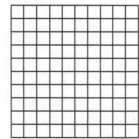 82% 20. 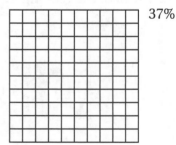 37%

21. **TEST SCORE** You take a test that has 20 questions and you get 80% of the questions correct. How many questions do you get correct? _____

22. **SALES TAX** You buy $50 worth of clothes. The sales tax is 8%. How much sales tax do you pay? _____

REVIEW: Percents and Fractions

Name _____

$$35\% = \frac{35}{100} = \frac{\cancel{5} \cdot 7}{\cancel{5} \cdot 20} = \frac{7}{20}$$

Write percent as a fraction in simplest form.

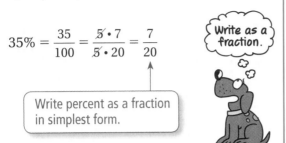

Write as a fraction.

Visual Model

$35\% = \dfrac{7}{20}$

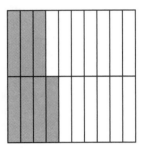

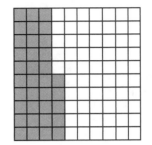

Skill Examples

1. $40\% = \dfrac{40}{100} = \dfrac{\cancel{20} \cdot 2}{\cancel{20} \cdot 5} = \dfrac{2}{5}$

2. $50\% = \dfrac{50}{100} = \dfrac{\cancel{50} \cdot 1}{\cancel{50} \cdot 2} = \dfrac{1}{2}$

3. $25\% = \dfrac{25}{100} = \dfrac{\cancel{25} \cdot 1}{\cancel{25} \cdot 4} = \dfrac{1}{4}$

4. $5\% = \dfrac{5}{100} = \dfrac{\cancel{5} \cdot 1}{\cancel{5} \cdot 20} = \dfrac{1}{20}$

Application Example

5. Your school's softball team won 30% of its games. Did the team win more than one-fourth of its games?

$$30\% = \frac{3}{10} \qquad \frac{3}{10} > \frac{1}{4}$$

Yes, the team won more than one-fourth of its games.

PRACTICE MAKES PURR-FECT™

Check your answers at BigIdeasMath.com.

Write the percent as a fraction in simplest form.

6. $20\% =$ _____

7. $45\% =$ _____

8. $7\% =$ _____

9. $32.5\% =$ _____

10. $15\% =$ _____

11. $1\% =$ _____

12. $150\% =$ _____

13. $33\frac{1}{3}\% =$ _____

Write the fraction as a percent.

14. $\dfrac{3}{20} =$ _____

15. $\dfrac{6}{5} =$ _____

16. $\dfrac{5}{8} =$ _____

17. $\dfrac{3}{5} =$ _____

Write the fraction represented by the model as a percent.

18.  _____

19.  _____

20. 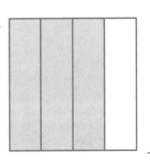 _____

21. **SURVEY** Eighteen out of twenty people in a survey said that vanilla ice cream is their favorite flavor of ice cream. What percent is this? _____

22. **SPANISH LANGUAGE** Twelve of the 40 students in your class can speak Spanish. What percent is this? _____

REVIEW: Percents and Decimals

Name _____

Key Concept and Vocabulary

$18\% = 0.18$ | **Percent to Decimal:** Move decimal point to the left 2 places.

$0.73 = 73\%$ | **Decimal to Percent:** Move decimal point to the right 2 places.

Visual Model

$18\% = 0.18$

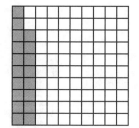 =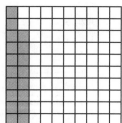

Skill Examples

1. $18\% = 0.18$

2. $145\% = 1.45$

3. $0.005 = 0.5\%$ *(one-half of one percent)*

4. $0.125 = 12.5\%$

Application Example

5. What percent of the circle graph is represented by the yellow region?

$0.36 = 36\%$

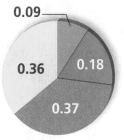

The yellow region is 36%.

PRACTICE MAKES PURR-FECT™

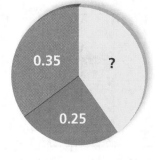

Check your answers at BigIdeasMath.com.

Write the percent as a decimal.

6. $20\% = $ _____   7. $45\% = $ _____   8. $7\% = $ _____   9. $32.5\% = $ _____

10. $15\% = $ _____   11. $1\% = $ _____   12. $150\% = $ _____   13. $0.2\% = $ _____

Write the decimal as a percent.

14. $0.13 = $ _____   15. $1.4 = $ _____   16. $0.001 = $ _____   17. $2.5 = $ _____

What percent of the circle graph is represented by the yellow region?

18.
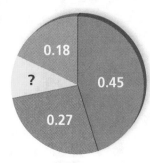
_____

19.

_____

20.

_____

21. **BUDGET** You have set aside two twenty-fifths of your monthly budget for clothing. What percent is this? _____

22. **SUMMER SCHOOL** Eighty-seven percent of the students in your class do not plan to attend summer school. What percent of your class plans to attend summer school? _____

REVIEW: Finding the Percent of a Number

Name _____

Key Concept and Vocabulary

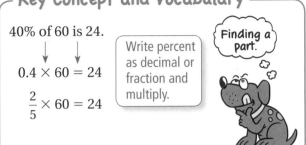

40% of 60 is 24.

$0.4 \times 60 = 24$

$\frac{2}{5} \times 60 = 24$

Write percent as decimal or fraction and multiply.

Finding a part.

Visual Model

0%	20%	40%	60%	80%	100%
0	12	24	36	48	60

Skill Examples

1. 30% of 50: $0.3 \times 50 = 15$

2. 45% of 80: $0.45 \times 80 = 36$

3. 110% of 40: $1.1 \times 40 = 44$

4. 25% of 240: $0.25 \times 240 = 60$

Application Example

5. 28% of the 200 people who answered a survey own a dog. How many of the 200 people in the survey own a dog?

$0.28 \times 200 = 56$

56 of the 200 people own a dog.

PRACTICE MAKES *PURR-FECT*™

Check your answers at BigIdeasMath.com.

Find the percent of the number.

6. 25% of 40 = _____ 7. 20% of 35 = _____ 8. 65% of 110 = _____ 9. 125% of 20 = _____

10. $33\frac{1}{3}$% of 60 = _____ 11. 95% of 400 = _____ 12. 200% of 31 = _____ 13. 18% of 90 = _____

14. 1% of 800 = _____ 15. 60% of 60 = _____ 16. 100% of 59 = _____ 17. 1000% of 59 = _____

Write the question represented by the model. Then answer the question.

18.
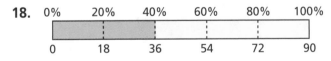

0%	20%	40%	60%	80%	100%
0	18	36	54	72	90

Question: _____

Answer: _____

19.
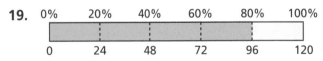

0%	20%	40%	60%	80%	100%
0	24	48	72	96	120

Question: _____

Answer: _____

20. **ENDANGERED SPECIES** Sixty percent of a species of butterfly died due to loss of habitat. Originally, there were 10,000 butterflies. How many are left? _____

21. **SALES TAX** You buy 4 breakfast sandwiches at $2.59 each, 4 hashbrowns at $1.10 each, and 4 bottles of orange juice at $1.25 each. The sales tax is 6%. Find the total cost of the 4 meals, including sales tax. _____

REVIEW: Perimeter

Name _____

Key Concept and Vocabulary

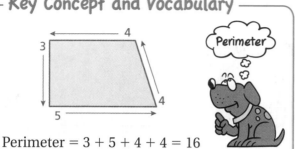

Perimeter

Perimeter = $3 + 5 + 4 + 4 = 16$

Visual Model

Perimeter = $10 + 9 + 11$

= 30

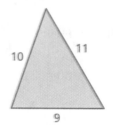

Skill Examples

1.

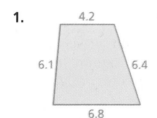

$P = 6.1 + 6.8 + 6.4 + 4.2$

= 23.5

2.

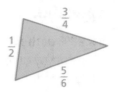

$P = \dfrac{1}{2} + \dfrac{5}{6} + \dfrac{3}{4}$

= $\dfrac{25}{12}$

Application Example

3. Find the length of fence needed to enclose the lot.

$P = 2(80) + 2(120)$

= $160 + 240$

= 400

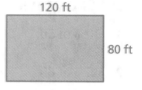

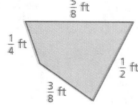 You need 400 feet of fence.

PRACTICE MAKES *PURR*-FECT™

Check your answers at BigIdeasMath.com. ━━━━

Find the perimeter of the figure.

4.

90 ft
65 ft

Perimeter = _____

5.

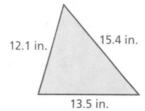

12.1 in.   15.4 in.
13.5 in.

Perimeter = _____

6.

$\frac{5}{8}$ ft
$\frac{1}{4}$ ft $\frac{1}{2}$ ft
$\frac{3}{8}$ ft

Perimeter = _____

7.

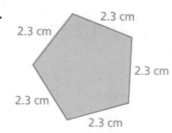

2.3 cm   2.3 cm
2.3 cm
2.3 cm
2.3 cm

Perimeter = _____

8.

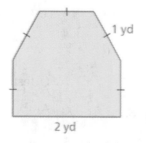

1 yd
2 yd

Perimeter = _____

9.

3 ft
2 ft

Perimeter = _____

10. RIBBON You are wrapping a ribbon around a rectangular box that is 18 inches long and 12 inches wide. What is the minimum amount of ribbon you need? _____

11. COUNTY LINE A county has the shape of a quadrilateral. The lengths of the four sides are 109 miles, 94 miles, 82 miles, and 109 miles. Find the perimeter of the county. _____

REVIEW: Area

Name _____

Key Concept and Vocabulary

Rectangle: $A = bh$

Parallelogram: $A = bh$

Triangle: $A = \frac{1}{2}bh$

Trapezoid: $A = \frac{1}{2}(B + b)h$

Visual Model

Area of a Rectangle:

$A = bh$

$\quad = (12)(10)$

$\quad = 120$ square units

height = 10

base = 12

Skill Examples

1.

1 cm

1 cm   1.2 cm

1.6 cm

$A = \frac{1}{2}(1.6 + 1)(1)$

$\quad = 1.3 \text{ cm}^2$

2.

2.4 in.

3.8 in.

$A = \frac{1}{2}(3.8)(2.4)$

$\quad = 4.56 \text{ in.}^2$

Application Example

3. Find the area of the apartment.

$A = 60 \cdot 40$

$\quad = 2400 \text{ ft}^2$

60 ft

40 ft

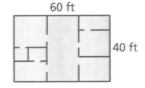

The area is 2400 square feet.

PRACTICE MAKES *PURR*-FECT™

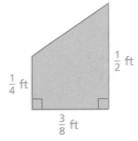

Check your answers at BigIdeasMath.com.

Find the area of the figure.

4.

50 ft

30 ft

Area = _____

5.

10.6 in.

13.5 in.

Area = _____

6.

$\frac{1}{2}$ ft

$\frac{1}{4}$ ft

$\frac{3}{8}$ ft

Area = _____

7.

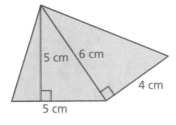

5 cm   6 cm

4 cm

5 cm

Area = _____

8.

8 yd

6 yd

2 yd

2 yd

Area = _____

9.

2 ft

$3\frac{1}{4}$ ft

Area = _____

10. CARPET You are carpeting a rectangular room that is 3.5 yards by 4.5 yards. The carpet costs $15 per square yard. How much will it cost to carpet the room? _____

11. COLORADO Colorado is approximately a rectangle that is 280 miles by 380 miles. Is the area of Colorado greater than or less than 100,000 square miles? Explain.

_____

REVIEW: Circles and Circumference

Name _____

Key Concept and Vocabulary

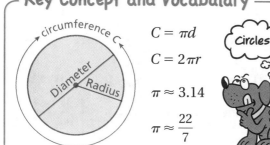

$C = \pi d$

$C = 2\pi r$

$\pi \approx 3.14$

$\pi \approx \dfrac{22}{7}$

Circles

Visual Model

Circumference of a Circle:

$$C = 2\pi r$$
$$= 2\pi(12)$$
$$= 24\pi$$
$$\approx 75.4$$

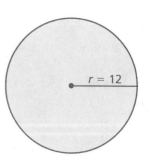

$r = 12$

Skill Examples

1.

$r = 2.4$ in.

$C = 2\pi(2.4)$
$= 4.8\pi$
≈ 15.1 in.

2.

$d = \frac{3}{4}$ ft

$C = \pi\left(\dfrac{3}{4}\right)$
≈ 2.4 ft

Application Example

3. Find the distance around the soccer ball.

$C = \pi(22.3)$
≈ 70.0 cm

22.3 cm

⠿ The distance is about 70 centimeters.

PRACTICE MAKES *PURR-FECT*™

Check your answers at BigIdeasMath.com.

Find the circumference. Round your answer to the nearest tenth.

4.
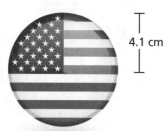
4.6 in.

Circumference ≈ _____

5.

7925 mi

Circumference ≈ _____

6.
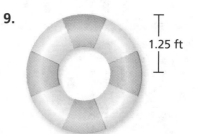
$2\frac{7}{8}$ in.

Circumference ≈ _____

7.
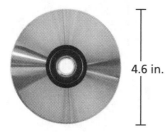
4.1 cm

Circumference ≈ _____

8.

0.42 in.

Circumference ≈ _____

9.

1.25 ft

Circumference ≈ _____

10. **RACETRACK** A circular racetrack has a circumference of one mile. What is the diameter of the racetrack in feet? _____

11. **OLD OAK TREE** You have 110 inches of yellow ribbon. The diameter of the old oak tree is 38 inches. Do you have enough yellow ribbon to wrap around the old oak tree? Explain.

_____

REVIEW: Areas of Circles

Name _____

Key Concept and Vocabulary

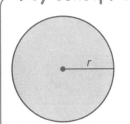

$A = \pi r^2$

$\pi \approx 3.14$

$\pi \approx \dfrac{22}{7}$

Area

Visual Model

Area of a Circle:

$$A = \pi r^2$$
$$= \pi(4)^2$$
$$= \pi(16)$$
$$\approx 50.2$$

 $r = 4$

Skill Examples

1.

 $r = 2.4$ in.

$A = \pi(2.4)^2$

≈ 18.1 in.^{2}

2.

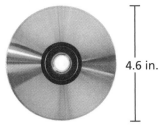 $d = \dfrac{3}{4}$ ft

$A = \pi\left(\dfrac{3}{8}\right)^2$

≈ 0.4 ft^2

Application Example

3. Find the area of a dime.

$A = \pi(0.9)^2$

≈ 2.5 cm^2

 1.8 cm

⁖ The area is about 2.5 square centimeters.

PRACTICE MAKES *PURR*-FECT™

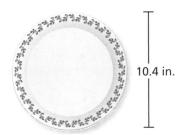

Check your answers at BigIdeasMath.com.

Find the area. Round your answer to the nearest tenth.

4.

 4.6 in.

Area ≈ _____

5.

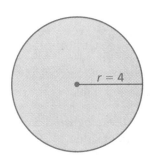 10.4 in.

Area ≈ _____

6.

2$\dfrac{7}{8}$ in.

Area ≈ _____

7.

 4.1 cm

Area ≈ _____

8.

 1.5 ft

Area ≈ _____

9.

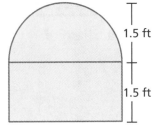 1.5 ft

1.5 ft

Area ≈ _____

10. BASKETBALL Find the area of the center circle on a basketball court. _____

11. BASKETBALL Find the area of a free throw region on a basketball court. _____

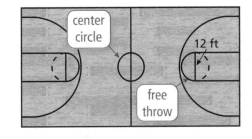

center circle

12 ft

free throw

REVIEW: Quadrilaterals

Name _____

Key Concept and Vocabulary

Quadrilateral	Diagram
A *trapezoid* has exactly 1 pair of parallel sides.	
A *parallelogram* has 2 pairs of parallel sides	
A *rectangle* is a parallelogram with 4 right angles.	
A *rhombus* is a parallelogram with 4 congruent sides.	
A *square* is a parallelogram with 4 right angles and 4 congruent sides.	

Classify.

Visual Model

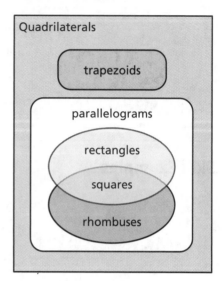

Skill Example

1. The quadrilateral has 4 right angles. The 4 sides are not congruent. The quadrilateral is a rectangle.

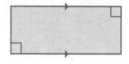

Application Example

2. The sum of the angle measures of a quadrilateral is 360°. Find the value of x in the rhombus.

$$x + 110 + 70 + 110 = 360$$
$$x + 290 = 360$$
$$x = 70$$

⋮⋮ The value of x is 70.

PRACTICE MAKES *PURR*-FECT™

Check your answers at BigIdeasMath.com.

Classify the quadrilateral.

3. 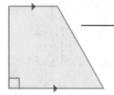 _____

4. _____

5. 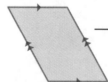 _____

6. **ANGLE MEASURE** Find the value of x in the quadrilateral. _____

7. **RHOMBUS** A quadrilateral has 4 right angles. Can the quadrilateral be classified as a rhombus? Explain.

_____

_____

REVIEW: Faces, Edges, and Vertices

Name _____

Key Concept and Vocabulary

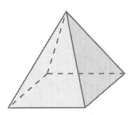

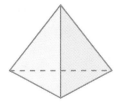

Polyhedra

Edge → Face →

Vertex →

$F + V = E + 2$

Visual Model

Rectangular Prism

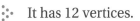

$F + V = E + 2$
$6 + 8 = 12 + 2$
$14 = 14$ ✓

6 Faces
12 Edges →
8 Vertices

Skill Examples

1.

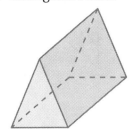

$F + V = E + 2$
$5 + 5 = 8 + 2$

2.

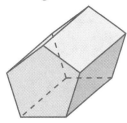

$F + V = E + 2$
$4 + 4 = 6 + 2$

Application Example

3. How many vertices does an icosahedron have?

$F + V = E + 2$
$20 + V = 30 + 2$
$V = 12$

It has 12 vertices.

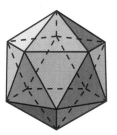

$F = 20$
$E = 30$

PRACTICE MAKES PURR-FECT™

Check your answers at BigIdeasMath.com.

Find the number of faces, edges, and vertices.

4. Triangular Prism

$F = $ ___, $E = $ ___, $V = $ ___

5. Pentagonal Prism

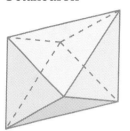

$F = $ ___, $E = $ ___, $V = $ ___

6. Octahedron

$F = $ ___, $E = $ ___, $V = $ ___

Find the missing number of faces, edges, or vertices.

7. Dodecahedron

$F = 12, E = 30, V = $ ___

8. Icosidodecahedron

$F = $ ___, $E = 60, V = 30$

9. Octagonal Prism

$F = 10, E = $ ___, $V = 16$

10. SOCCER BALL A soccer ball has the shape of a truncated icosahedron. It has 32 faces and 90 edges.

a. How many vertices does it have? _____

b. The vertices of an icosahedron are cut off to form the pentagons and hexagons seen on the soccer ball. How many of the faces are pentagons? _____

REVIEW: Surface Areas of Prisms

Name _____

Key Concept and Vocabulary

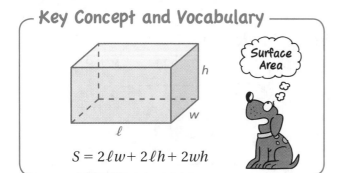

$$S = 2\ell w + 2\ell h + 2wh$$

Visual Model

Net for a Rectangular Prism

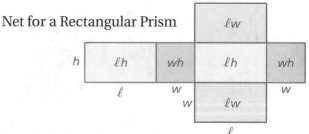

Skill Example

1.

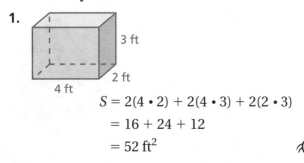

$$S = 2(4 \cdot 2) + 2(4 \cdot 3) + 2(2 \cdot 3)$$
$$= 16 + 24 + 12$$
$$= 52 \text{ ft}^2$$

Application Example

2. Find the surface area of the block.

$$S = 2\left(\frac{1}{2} \cdot 3 \cdot 4\right) + 4 \cdot 5 + 3 \cdot 4 + 4 \cdot 4$$
$$= 12 + 20 + 12 + 16$$
$$= 60 \text{ cm}^2$$

∴ The area is 60 cm².

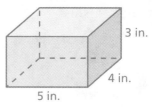

PRACTICE MAKES *PURR*-FECT™

Check your answers at BigIdeasMath.com. ▬

Find the surface area of the prism.

3. Rectangular Prism

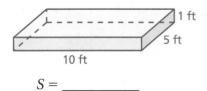

$S =$ _____

4. Rectangular Prism

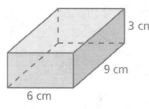

$S =$ _____

5. Rectangular Prism

$S =$ _____

6. Triangular Prism

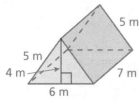

$S =$ _____

7. Triangular Prism

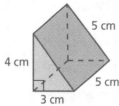

$S =$ _____

8. Triangular Prism

$S =$ _____

9. **AQUARIUM** How much glass is used to make the four sides of the aquarium?_____

10. **AQUARIUM** How much glass is used to make the base of the aquarium? _____

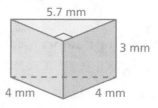

REVIEW: Surface Areas of Cylinders

Name _____

Visual Model

Net for a
Circular Cylinder

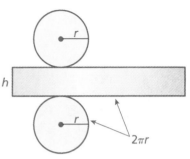

Skill Example

1.

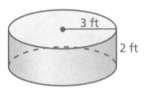

$$S = 2\pi \cdot 3^2 + 2\pi \cdot 3 \cdot 2$$
$$= 18\pi + 12\pi$$
$$= 30\pi \, \text{ft}^2$$

Application Example

2. Find the surface area of
the soup can.

$$S = 2\pi \cdot 1.5^2 + 2\pi \cdot 1.5 \cdot 5$$
$$= 4.5\pi + 15\pi$$
$$= 19.5\pi \, \text{in.}^2$$

∴ The area is 19.5π square inches.

PRACTICE MAKES *PURR-FECT*™

Check your answers at BigIdeasMath.com.

Find the surface area of the circular cylinder.

3. Circular Cylinder

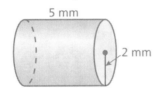

$S =$ _____

4. Circular Cylinder

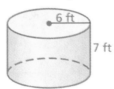

$S =$ _____

5. Circular Cylinder

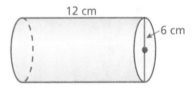

$S =$ _____

6. Circular Cylinder

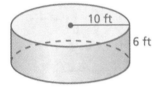

$S =$ _____

7. Circular Cylinder

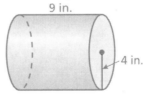

$S =$ _____

8. Circular Cylinder

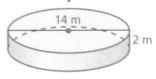

$S =$ _____

9. OIL TANKER TRUCK The truck's tank is a stainless steel
cylinder. How many square feet of stainless steel are
needed to make the tank? _____

10. OIL TANKER TRUCK What percent of the stainless steel in
the tank is used to make the two ends? _____

Length = 50 ft
Radius = 4 ft

REVIEW: Surface Areas of Pyramids and Cones

Name _____

Key Concept and Vocabulary

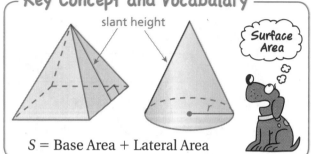

slant height

$S = $ Base Area + Lateral Area

Visual Model

Net for a Square Pyramid

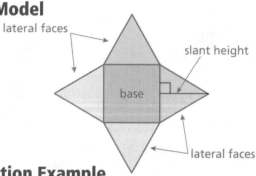

lateral faces

slant height

base

lateral faces

Skill Example

1. Cone

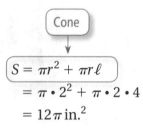

$\ell = 4$ in.

$r = 2$ in.

$$S = \pi r^2 + \pi r \ell$$
$$= \pi \cdot 2^2 + \pi \cdot 2 \cdot 4$$
$$= 12\pi \text{ in.}^2$$

Application Example

2. Find the lateral surface area of the square pyramid.

$$S = 4\left(\frac{1}{2} \cdot 40 \cdot 35\right)$$
$$= 2800 \text{ m}^2$$

35 m

40 m

The area is 2800 square meters.

PRACTICE MAKES *PURR-FECT*™

Check your answers at BigIdeasMath.com.

Find the surface area of the pyramid or cone.

3. Square Pyramid

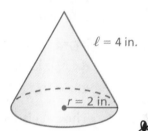

8 in.

5 in.

$S = $ _____

4. Square Pyramid

9 ft

6 ft

$S = $ _____

5. Square Pyramid

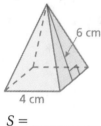

6 cm

4 cm

$S = $ _____

6. Cone

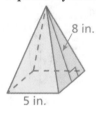

6 in.

3 in.

$S = $ _____

7. Cone

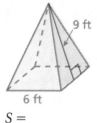

5 m

4 m

$S = $ _____

8. Cone

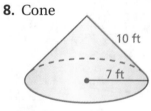

10 ft

7 ft

$S = $ _____

9. VOLCANO Find the lateral surface area of the volcano. Use 3.14 for π. Round your answer to the nearest hundred square feet. _____

10. VOLCANO Find the area of the circular region covered by the base of the volcano. Use 3.14 for π. Round your answer to the nearest hundred square feet. _____

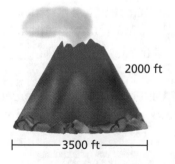

2000 ft

3500 ft

REVIEW: Volumes of Prisms

Name _____

Key Concept and Vocabulary

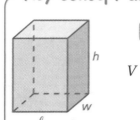

 Base

$V = Bh$
$\quad = \ell wh$

 Volume

Visual Model

Volume of a
Rectangular Prism

$V = 2 \cdot 4 \cdot 3$
$\quad = 24 \text{ units}^3$

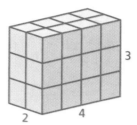

Skill Example

1.

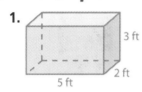

3 ft
2 ft
5 ft

$V = 5 \cdot 2 \cdot 3$
$\quad = 30 \text{ ft}^3$

Application Example

2. Find the volume of the block.

$V = Bh$

$\quad = \left(\dfrac{1}{2} \cdot 3 \cdot 4\right) \cdot 5$

$\quad = 30 \text{ cm}^3$

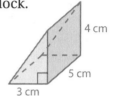

4 cm
5 cm
3 cm

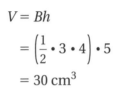 The volume is 30 cubic centimeters.

PRACTICE MAKES PURR-FECT™

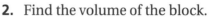

Check your answers at BigIdeasMath.com.

Find the volume of the prism.

3. Rectangular Prism

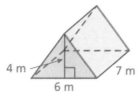

1 ft
5 ft
10 ft

$V =$ _____

4. Rectangular Prism

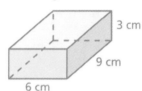

3 cm
9 cm
6 cm

$V =$ _____

5. Rectangular Prism

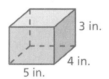

3 in.
4 in.
5 in.

$V =$ _____

6. Triangular Prism

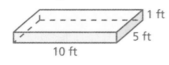

4 m
6 m
7 m

$V =$ _____

7. Triangular Prism

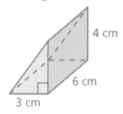

4 cm
6 cm
3 cm

$V =$ _____

8. Triangular Prism

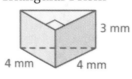

3 mm
4 mm
4 mm

$V =$ _____

9. AQUARIUM How much water is needed to fill the aquarium? _____

10. AQUARIUM There are about 7.5 gallons in 1 cubic foot. How many gallons of water does the aquarium hold? _____

2 ft
1.5 ft
4 ft

REVIEW: Volumes of Cylinders

Name _____

Key Concept and Vocabulary

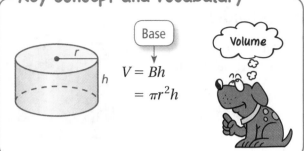

$$V = Bh$$
$$= \pi r^2 h$$

Visual Model

If each coin has a volume of πr^2, then h coins have a volume of

$$V = \pi r^2 h.$$

Skill Example

1.

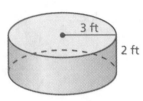

3 ft

2 ft

$$V = \pi \cdot 3^2 \cdot 2$$
$$= 18\pi \text{ ft}^3$$

Application Example

2. How much soup is in the can?

$$V = \pi \cdot 1.5^2 \cdot 5$$
$$= 11.25\pi \text{ in.}^3$$

├─3 in.─┤

5 in.

There are 11.25π cubic inches of soup.

PRACTICE MAKES *PURR*-FECT™

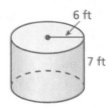

Check your answers at BigIdeasMath.com.

Find the volume of the circular cylinder.

3. Circular Cylinder

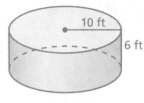

5 mm

2 mm

$V =$ _____

4. Circular Cylinder

6 ft

7 ft

$V =$ _____

5. Circular Cylinder

12 cm

6 cm

$V =$ _____

6. Circular Cylinder

10 ft

6 ft

$V =$ _____

7. Circular Cylinder

9 in.

4 in.

$V =$ _____

8. Circular Cylinder

14 m

2 m

$V =$ _____

9. **OIL TANKER TRUCK** The truck's tank is a stainless steel cylinder. How much oil does the tank hold? _____

10. **OIL TANKER TRUCK** There are about 7.5 gallons in 1 cubic foot. How many gallons of oil can the tank hold? _____

Length = 50 ft
Radius = 4 ft

REVIEW: Volumes of Pyramids

Name _____

Key Concept and Vocabulary

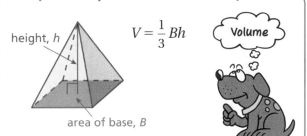

height, h

area of base, B

$V = \frac{1}{3}Bh$

Volume

Visual Model

The volume of a pyramid is *one-third* the volume of the prism that has the same base and height.

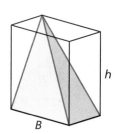

h

B

Skill Example

1.
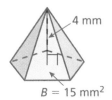

7 in.

8 in.

10 in.

$V = \frac{1}{3}Bh$

$= \frac{1}{3} \cdot (8 \cdot 10) \cdot 7$

$= \frac{560}{3}$

$= 186\frac{2}{3}$ in.^{3}

Application Example

2. Find the volume of the square pyramid.

$V = \frac{1}{3} \cdot (40^2) \cdot 30$

$= 16,000$ m^3

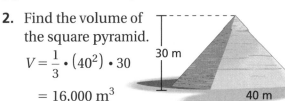

30 m

40 m

The volume is 16,000 cubic meters.

PRACTICE MAKES *PURR-FECT*™

Check your answers at BigIdeasMath.com.

Find the volume of the pyramid.

3.
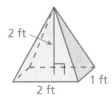

2 ft

2 ft   1 ft

$V = $ _____

4.
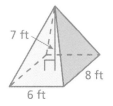

4 mm

$B = 15$ mm^2

$V = $ _____

5.
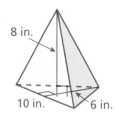

8 in.

10 in.   6 in.

$V = $ _____

6.
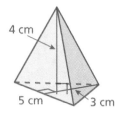

4 cm

5 cm   3 cm

$V = $ _____

7.

7 ft

8 ft

6 ft

$V = $ _____

8.
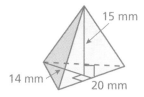

15 mm

14 mm   20 mm

$V = $ _____

9. **PYRAMID** The pyramid has a volume of 2000 cubic feet. Find a set of possible dimensions for the pyramid.

$w = $ _____, $\ell = $ _____, $h = $ _____

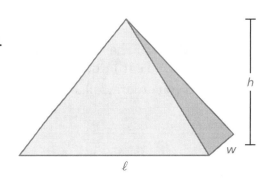

h

w

ℓ

REVIEW: Volumes of Cones

Name _____

Key Concept and Vocabulary

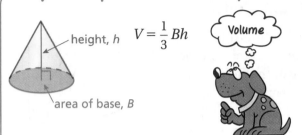

height, h

$V = \dfrac{1}{3} Bh$

Volume

area of base, B

Visual Model

The volume of a cone is *one-third* the volume of the cylinder that has the same base and height.

h

B

Skill Example

1.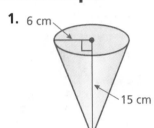

6 cm

15 cm

$V = \dfrac{1}{3} Bh$

$= \dfrac{1}{3} \cdot (\pi \cdot 6^2) \cdot 15$

$= 180\pi \text{ cm}^3$

Application Example

2. How much water does the funnel hold?

$V = \dfrac{1}{3} \cdot (\pi \cdot 3^2) \cdot 5$

$= 15\pi \text{ in.}^3$

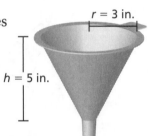

$r = 3$ in.

$h = 5$ in.

∴ It holds 15π cubic inches.

PRACTICE MAKES *PURR*-FECT™

Check your answers at BigIdeasMath.com.

Find the volume of the cone.

3.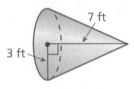

7 ft

3 ft

$V = $ _____

4.

4 in.

2 in.

$V = $ _____

5.

3 m

6 m

$V = $ _____

6.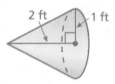

2 ft

1 ft

$V = $ _____

7.

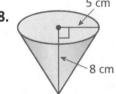

10 mm

5 mm

$V = $ _____

8.

5 cm

8 cm

$V = $ _____

9. **LEMONADE** You have 10 gallons of lemonade (1 gal ≈ 3785 cm³) How many of the paper cups should you order? Explain. _____

_____

_____

8 cm

11 cm

Key Concept and Vocabulary

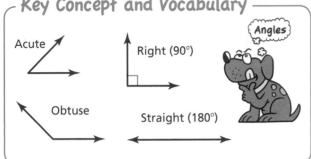

Acute

Right (90°)

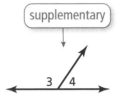
Angles

Obtuse

Straight (180°)

Visual Model

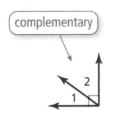
complementary

2

1

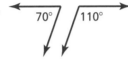
supplementary

3 4

Skill Examples

1.

49°
41°

41° + 49° = 90°
complementary

2.

70° 110°

70° + 110° = 180°
supplementary

Application Example

3. Find the measures of angles 1, 2, and 3.

95
50°
80
1
3
2
80
95

∠1 = 130°
∠2 = 50°
∠3 = 130°

PRACTICE MAKES PURR-FECT™

Check your answers at BigIdeasMath.com.

Decide whether the angles are *complementary*, *supplementary*, or *neither*.

4.

42°
48°

_____

5.

45°
55°

_____

6.

59° 31°

_____

7.

115° 65°

_____

8.

156°
24°

_____

9.

122° 68°

_____

Find the value of *x*. State whether the angle of *x* is *acute*, *right*, *obtuse*, or *straight*.

10.

x°
35°

x = _____

11.

x°
128°

x = _____

12.

117° *x*°

x = _____

13. TRIBUTARY A tributary joins a river at an angle of *x*°. Find the value of *x*. _____

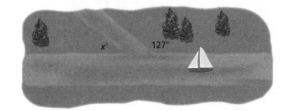
x° 127°

REVIEW: Similar Figures

Name _____

Key Concept and Vocabulary

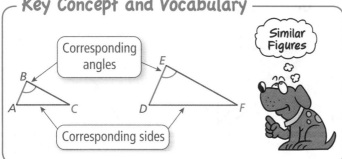

Corresponding angles

Corresponding sides

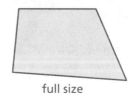

Similar Figures

Visual Model

Similar figures are the same shape, but not necessarily the same size.

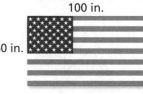

full size   half size

Skill Example

1. **Similar Triangles**

$$\frac{9}{6} = \frac{12}{8} = \frac{6}{4}$$

Ratios of corresponding sides are equal.

 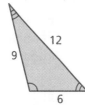

Application Example

2. Are the two flags similar?

$$\frac{60}{35} \neq \frac{100}{50}$$

They are not similar.

100 in.

60 in.

50 in.

35 in.

PRACTICE MAKES PURR-FECT™

Check your answers at BigIdeasMath.com.

Decide whether the two figures are similar.

3.
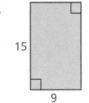

15

6

9

9

4.
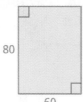

80

60

60

45

5.
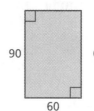

90

60

60

45

6.
 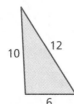

8

6

4

10

12

6

7.
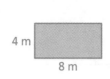 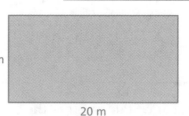

4 m

8 m

10 m

20 m

8. **TENNIS COURTS** Are the two tennis courts similar? Explain. _____

Singles

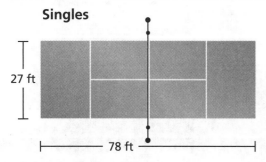

27 ft

78 ft

Doubles

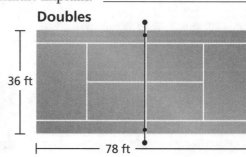

36 ft

78 ft

REVIEW: Line Symmetry

Name _____

Key Concept and Vocabulary

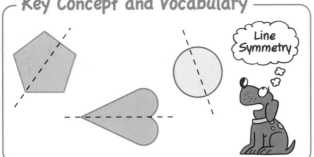

Line Symmetry

Visual Model

If a figure has line symmetry, you can fold it on the line of symmetry and the figure will coincide with itself.

Skill Examples

1.

Not line symmetry

2.

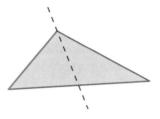

Not line symmetry

Application Example

3. Is the house on the right identical to the house on the left?

  They are identical, but flipped over.

PRACTICE MAKES *PURR-FECT*™

Check your answers at BigIdeasMath.com.

Draw all lines of symmetry on the figure. If none, write "none."

4. Isosceles Trapezoid

5. Parallelogram

6. Ellipse

7. Isosceles Triangle

8. Rectangle

9. Square

10. **CLOWN** Which clown face has line symmetry? _____

(a)

(b)

(c)

REVIEW: Rotational Symmetry

Name _____

Key Concept and Vocabulary

Rotate about point *P*.

Visual Model

If a figure has rotational symmetry, you can rotate it about a point and the figure will coincide with itself.

(Rotate this worksheet 180°. The word will be the same.)

Skill Examples

1.

Rotational symmetry 120°, 240°

2.

Rotational symmetry 90°, 180°, 270°

Application Example

3. Why are traditional playing cards made with rotational symmetry?

⋮ So that when you rotate them 180°, you see the same picture.

PRACTICE MAKES *PURR-FECT*™

Check your answers at BigIdeasMath.com.

List the angles (less than 360°) that represent rotational symmetry.

4. Equilateral Triangle

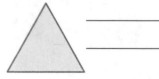   _____
   _____

5. Square

   _____
   _____

6. Regular Pentagon

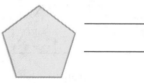   _____
   _____

7. Regular Hexagon

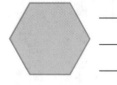   _____
   _____
   _____

8. Rectangle

   _____
   _____

9. Equilateral Trapezoid

   _____
   _____

10. **AMBIGRAM** A rotational ambigram is a word that has rotational symmetry. Which of the following ambigrams contain the same word when rotated? _____

(a)

(b) **WOW**

(c) *Symmetry*

REVIEW: Mean, Median, and Mode

Name _____

Key Concept and Vocabulary

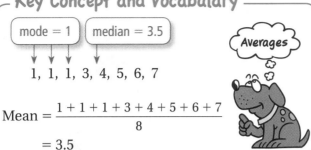

mode = 1   median = 3.5

Averages

1, 1, 1, 3, 4, 5, 6, 7

$$\text{Mean} = \frac{1+1+1+3+4+5+6+7}{8}$$

$$= 3.5$$

Visual Model

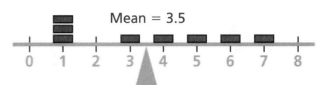

Mean = 3.5

The scale balances at the mean.

Skill Example

1.
mode = 1   median = 4

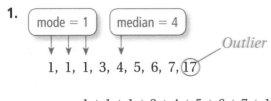

Outlier

1, 1, 1, 3, 4, 5, 6, 7, (17)

$$\text{Mean} = \frac{1+1+1+3+4+5+6+7+17}{9}$$

$$= 5$$

Application Example

2. What is the mean weight of the bowling balls?

$13 + 12 + 9 + 10 + 13 + 9 = 66$

$$\text{Mean} = \frac{66}{6} = 11$$

The mean is 11 pounds.

PRACTICE MAKES *PURR-FECT*™

Check your answers at BigIdeasMath.com.

Find the mean, median, and mode of the data.

3. 2, 6, 9, 10, 3, 4, 6, 12, 4, 13

Mean = ____, Median = ____, Mode = _____

4. 30, 48, 32, 43, 45, 32

Mean = ____, Median = ____, Mode = _____

5. 18, 12, 25, 18, 17, 19, 29, 20, 13, 18

Mean = ____, Median = ____, Mode = _____

6. 6.8, 6.2, 6.3, 6.8, 5.9, 6.0, 6.1, 5.9

Mean = ____, Median = ____, Mode = _____

7. −4, 5, 3, −2, 1, 0, −2

Mean = ____, Median = ____, Mode = _____

8. 2, 5, 5, 0, 12, 5, 7, 8, 12, 9

Mean = ____, Median = ____, Mode = _____

9. SALARIES The weekly salaries of six employees at a fast-food restaurant are $140, $220, $90, $180, $140, and $200. Find the mean, median, and mode of these salaries.

Mean = _____, Median = _____, Mode = _____

10. PUPPIES A litter of puppies is 8 weeks old. Find the mean, median, and mode weights of the puppies.

Mean = _____, Median = _____, Mode = _____

 5.1 lb   5.2 lb   5.4 lb   6.0 lb

3.7 lb   5.5 lb   4.8 lb

REVIEW: Circle Graphs

Name _____

Key Concept and Vocabulary

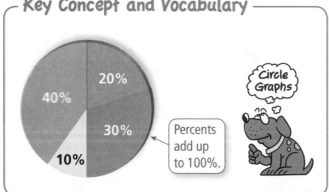

Percents add up to 100%.

Visual Model

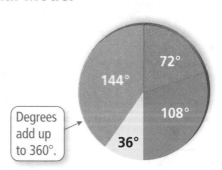

Degrees add up to 360°.

Skill Example

1. Data: 15, 15, 30

   Angles:

   $\frac{15}{60} = 25\% \longrightarrow 90°$

   $\frac{30}{60} = 50\% \longrightarrow 180°$

Application Example

2. 200 people were asked their favorite color. How many said blue?

   20% of 200 = 40

   ⋮ 40 people said "blue."

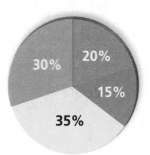

PRACTICE MAKES *PURR*-FECT™

Check your answers at BigIdeasMath.com.

Draw a circle graph for the data. Label each part of the graph.

3. Favorite Pet:
   dog 9, cat 5,
   fish 3, bird 1

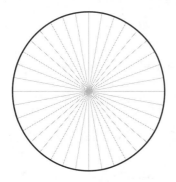

4. Favorite Day:
   Friday 9,
   Saturday 12,
   Sunday 15

BUDGET A family is making a monthly budget. Its total take-home pay for a month is $2400.

5. How much is budgeted for food? _____

6. How much is budgeted for miscellaneous? _____

7. How much is budgeted for rent? _____

8. How much is budgeted for clothes? _____

9. How much is budgeted for savings? _____

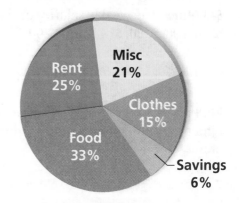

REVIEW: Bar Graphs

Name _____

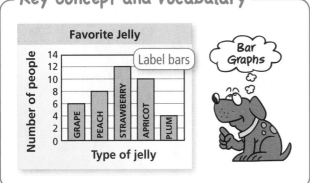
Visual Model

Favorite Jellies

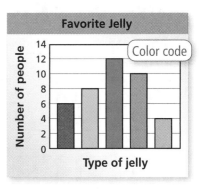

- Grape 6
- Peach 8
- Strawberry 12
- Apricot 10
- Plum 4

Skill Example

1. **Data**

   Cats 6

   Dogs 8

   Birds 3

   Fish 2

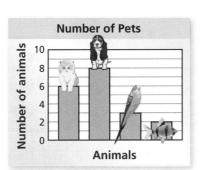

Application Example

2. How many people said they slept 8 hours a night?

   ∴ 30 people

PRACTICE MAKES *PURR*-FECT™

Check your answers at BigIdeasMath.com.

Draw a bar graph for the data. Label each part of the graph.

3. Hours Worked:
   Mon: 8, Tue: 7, Wed: 10, Thu: 10, Fri: 6

4. Hours Slept:
   Mon: 8, Tue: 7, Wed: 6, Thu: 9, Fri: 7

CONTEST A class held an ice cream eating contest. The finalist scores are shown in the bar graph.

5. How many scoops did John eat? _____

6. How many scoops did Amy eat? _____

7. How many scoops did Juan eat? _____

8. How many scoops did Chu eat? _____

9. How many scoops did Fred eat? _____

REVIEW: Frequency Tables

Name _____

Key Concept and Vocabulary

Number	Tally	Frequency
1	IIII	4
2	ЖГ	5
3	III	3
4	III	3
5	II	2

Frequency Tables

Visual Model

A *histogram* shows the frequency of data values in intervals of the same size.

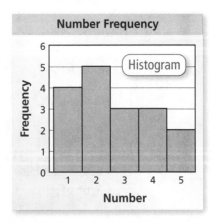

Skill Example

1. **Data:** 4, 6, 3, 6, 4, 5, 5, 6, 3, 5, 6, 3, 5, 6

Number	Tally	Frequency
3	III	3
4	II	2
5	IIII	4
6	ЖГ	5

Application Example

2. How many 12-year-olds attended the swimming event?

   ⋰ about 13

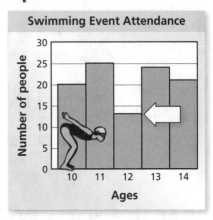

PRACTICE MAKES *PURR-FECT*™

Check your answers at BigIdeasMath.com.

Make a frequency table for the data. Then draw a histogram for the data.

3. **Data (Ages)**
   5, 5, 7, 8, 4, 7, 5,
   6, 7, 8, 4, 6, 6, 5,
   7, 7, 6, 6, 7, 4, 8,
   4, 6, 6, 5, 5, 7, 6

Number	Tally	Frequency
4		
5		
6		
7		
8		

BIRTH WEIGHT The histogram shows the birth weights for babies at a hospital.

4. How many babies weigh 6 pounds? _____

5. How many weigh 7 pounds? _____

6. How many weigh less than 6 pounds? _____

7. How many weigh 6 or more pounds? _____

8. Approximate the mean birth weight. _____

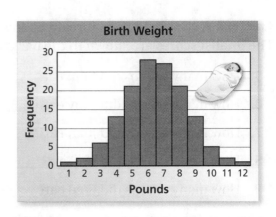

Name _____

Key Concept and Vocabulary

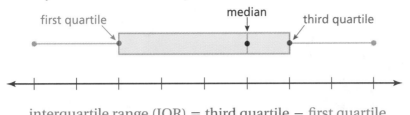

interquartile range (IQR) = third quartile − first quartile

An outlier is any data value that is:

- less than first quartile − 1.5 × IQR
- greater than third quartile + 1.5 × IQR

Half of the data values lie in the box.

Skill Example

1.

lower half   upper half

10 21 21 23   25 26 28 42

first quartile, 21   third quartile, 27

IQR = 27 − 21 = 6

21 − 1.5 × 6 = 12   27 + 1.5 × 6 = 36

Because 10 < 12, 10 is an outlier.

Because 42 > 36, 42 is an outlier.

Application Example

2. The table shows the heights of seven students. Identify any outlier(s).

Height (in inches)						
52	47	55	81	61	49	59

Order the data: 47, 49, 52, 55, 59, 61, 81

IQR = 61 − 49 = 12

49 − 1.5 × 12 = 31   61 + 1.5 × 12 = 79

Because 81 > 79, 81 is an outlier. There are no data values less than 31.

PRACTICE MAKES *PURR-FECT*™

Check your answers at BigIdeasMath.com.

Find the interquartile range.

3.

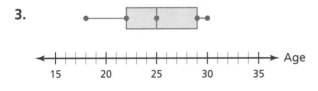

_____

4.

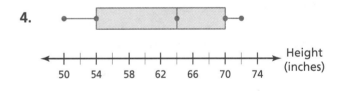

_____

Identify any outlier(s) of the data set.

5. 8, 10, 13, 13, 14, 16, 27 _____

6. 20, 22, 22, 25, 28, 32, 34, 43 _____

7. 44, 51, 36, 19, 40, 69, 49, 46 _____

8. 76, 72, 64, 93, 80, 78, 96, 75, 70, 72 _____

9. **BASKETBALL** The table shows the free throw percentage of each player on a basketball team. Identify any outlier(s). _____

Free Throw Percentage			
75	72	54	69
82	51	74	76
79	85	75	84

REVIEW: Converting Customary Units   Name _____

Key Concept and Vocabulary

Length
1 ft = 12 in.
1 yd = 3 ft
1 mi = 5280 ft

Weight
1 lb = 16 oz
1 ton = 2000 lb

Volume
1 Tbsp = 3 tsp
1 fl oz = 2 Tbsp
1 cup = 16 Tbsp
1 cup = 8 fl oz
1 pt = 2 cups
1 qt = 4 cups
1 gal = 4 qt

Customary Units

Visual Model

gallon

half gallon

quart

pint

cup

Skill Examples

1. $3 \text{ ft} = 3 \text{ ft} \cdot \dfrac{12 \text{ in.}}{1 \text{ ft}} = 36 \text{ in.}$

2. $1.5 \text{ mi} = 1.5 \text{ mi} \cdot \dfrac{5280 \text{ ft}}{1 \text{ mi}} = 7920 \text{ ft}$

3. $2\dfrac{1}{4} \text{ lb} = 2\dfrac{1}{4} \text{ lb} \cdot \dfrac{16 \text{ oz}}{1 \text{ lb}} = 36 \text{ oz}$

4. $5 \text{ qt} = 5 \text{ qt} \cdot \dfrac{4 \text{ cups}}{1 \text{ qt}} = 20 \text{ cups}$

Application Example

5. A typical SUV weighs about 2.5 tons. How many pounds is that?

$2.5 \text{ tons} = 2.5 \text{ tons} \cdot \dfrac{2000 \text{ lb}}{1 \text{ ton}}$

It is 5000 pounds.

PRACTICE MAKES PURR-FECT™

Check your answers at BigIdeasMath.com.

Complete the unit conversion.

6. 3 mi = _____ ft

7. 3 in. = _____ ft

8. $\dfrac{1}{4}$ mi = _____ ft

9. 4 ft = _____ yd

10. 4 ft = _____ in.

11. 1760 yd = _____ mi

12. 32 oz = _____ lb

13. $\dfrac{3}{4}$ ton = _____ lb

14. 2.5 lb = _____ oz

15. 6 cups = _____ qt

16. 2 cups = _____ fl oz

17. 64 oz = _____ gal

RECIPES Find the number of cups and the number of fluid ounces.

18.

_____ cups = _____ fl oz

19.

_____ cups = _____ fl oz

20.

_____ cups = _____ fl oz

21. **SPEED** A parachutist falls at a speed of about 12 miles per hour. Find this speed in feet per second. _____

REVIEW: Converting Metric Units

Name _____

Key Concept and Vocabulary

Length
$1 \text{ cm} = 10 \text{ mm}$
$1 \text{ m} = 100 \text{ cm}$
$1 \text{ km} = 1000 \text{ m}$

Weight (Mass)
$1 \text{ g} = 1000 \text{ mg}$
$1 \text{ kg} = 1000 \text{ g}$

Volume
$1 \text{ L} = 1000 \text{ mL}$
$1 \text{ kL} = 1000 \text{ L}$
$1 \text{ cm}^3 = 1 \text{ mL}$
$1 \text{ L} = 1000 \text{ cm}^3$
$1 \text{ m}^3 = 1000 \text{ L}$
$1 \text{ m}^3 = 1,000,000 \text{ cm}^3$

Metric Units

Visual Model

1 liter $\approx$ 1 quart $+ \dfrac{1}{4}$ cup

Skill Examples

1. $3 \text{ m} = 3 \text{ m} \cdot \dfrac{100 \text{ cm}}{1 \text{ m}} = 300 \text{ cm}$

2. $0.75 \text{ km} = 0.75 \text{ km} \cdot \dfrac{1000 \text{ m}}{1 \text{ km}} = 750 \text{ m}$

3. $50 \text{ mg} = 50 \text{ mg} \cdot \dfrac{1 \text{ g}}{1000 \text{ mg}} = 0.05 \text{ g}$

4. $750 \text{ mL} = 750 \text{ mL} \cdot \dfrac{1 \text{ L}}{1000 \text{ mL}} = 0.75 \text{ L}$

Application Example

5. A runner is running in a 100 meter dash. How many kilometers is that?

$100 \text{ m} = 100 \text{ m} \cdot \dfrac{1 \text{ km}}{1000 \text{ m}}$

$= 0.1 \text{ km}$

⋮ It is one-tenth of a kilometer.

PRACTICE MAKES *PURR*-FECT™

Check your answers at BigIdeasMath.com.

Complete the unit conversion.

6. $30 \text{ cm} = $ _____ m

7. $30 \text{ cm} = $ _____ mm

8. $0.5 \text{ km} = $ _____ m

9. $2 \text{ m} = $ _____ cm

10. $1500 \text{ cm} = $ _____ m

11. $1000 \text{ mm} = $ _____ m

12. $250 \text{ g} = $ _____ kg

13. $0.75 \text{ kg} = $ _____ g

14. $500 \text{ mg} = $ _____ g

15. $2 \text{ L} = $ _____ mL

16. $4000 \text{ mL} = $ _____ L

17. $500 \text{ cm}^3 = $ _____ mL

METRIC AND CUSTOMARY CONVERSION Use the conversion 1 in. $\approx$ 2.54 cm.

18.

|← 4 in. →|

Salamander length $\approx$ _____ cm

19.

|← 8 cm →|

Flower length $\approx$ _____ in.

20.

|← 6.5 in. →|

Toy car length $\approx$ _____ cm

21. **SPEED** One mile is about 1.6 kilometers. What is the speed limit in kilometers per hour?

_____

SPEED LIMIT 65 mph

REVIEW: Using a Compass

Name _____

Visual Model **Drawing a circle**

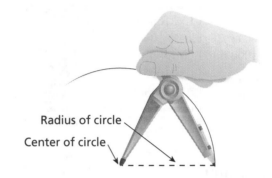

Radius of circle

Center of circle

Skill Example

1. Copy the segment.

a.

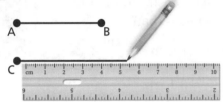

A •————————• B

C •

b.

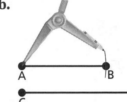

A •————————• B

C •————————

c.

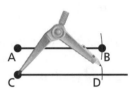

A •————————• B

C •————————• D

AB and *CD* have the same length.

PRACTICE MAKES *PURR*-FECT™

Check your answers at BigIdeasMath.com.

Use a straightedge and compass to copy the segment.

2. •————————————•

3. •————————————————————————————•

4. Draw a circle that has a radius of 3 centimeters.

5. Set the compass to a length of 1 inch. Complete the triangle so that it has sides of 4 inches, 3 inches, and 5 inches.

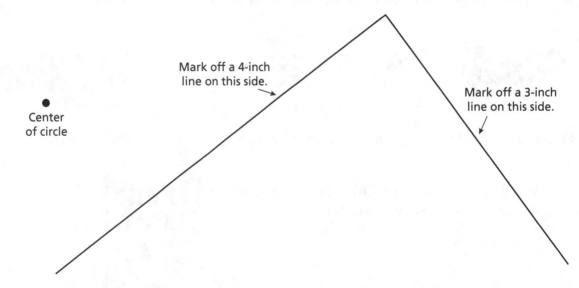

Mark off a 4-inch line on this side.

Mark off a 3-inch line on this side.

• Center of circle

REVIEW: Using a Protractor

Name _____

Key Concept and Vocabulary

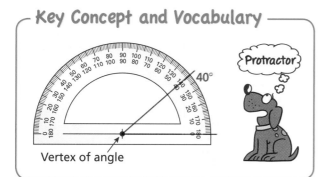

40°

Vertex of angle

Protractor

Visual Model

Protractors have 2 sets of numbers in opposite directions. When in doubt as to which to use, think "*Should this angle be greater than or less than than 90°?*"

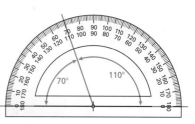

70°   110°

Skill Example

1. Measure an angle in a triangle.

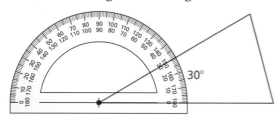

30°

Application Example

2. Measure the pitch angle of the roof.

Pitch angle   Pitch angle

⋮➤ The angle is about 20°.

PRACTICE MAKES *PURR*-FECT™

Check your answers at BigIdeasMath.com.

Draw an angle that has the given degree measure.

3. 35°

4. 60°

Vertex of angle

●—————————————————

Vertex of angle

Measure each angle of the triangle. Check that the total is 180°.

5. A = _____
   B = _____
   C = _____

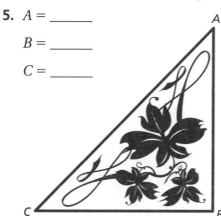

A

C   B

6. A = _____
   B = _____
   C = _____

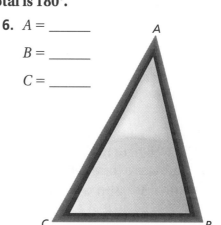

A

C   B

REVIEW: Evaluating Expressions

Name _____

Key Concept and Vocabulary

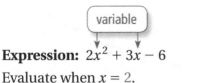
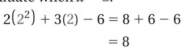

variable

Expression: $2x^2 + 3x - 6$

Evaluate when $x = 2$.

$2(2^2) + 3(2) - 6 = 8 + 6 - 6$
$= 8$

Visual Model

x	2x + 3	Value of Expression
1	$2(1) + 3$	5
2	$2(2) + 3$	7
3	$2(3) + 3$	9
4	$2(4) + 3$	11

Skill Examples

1. When $x = 5$, $3x + 4$ is $3(5) + 4 = 19$.

2. When $x = -1$, $5x + 7$ is $5(-1) + 7 = 2$.

3. When $x = 3$, $4x^2$ is $4(3^2) = 36$.

4. When $x = 4$, $x^3 + 1$ is $4^3 + 1 = 65$.

Application Example

5. For a Celsius temperature C the Fahrenheit temperature F is $\frac{9}{5}C + 32$. Find F when $C = 25°$.

$$\frac{9}{5}C + 32 = \frac{9}{5}(25) + 32$$
$$= 45 + 32$$
$$= 77$$

⋮ The Fahrenheit temperature is $77°$.

PRACTICE MAKES *PURR*-FECT™

Check your answers at BigIdeasMath.com.

Evaluate the expression.

6. When $x = 2$, $3x - 1 =$ _____.

7. When $x = -1$, $3x + 9 =$ _____.

8. When $x = 4$, $x^2 - 5 =$ _____.

9. When $x = \frac{1}{2}$, $3x^2 =$ _____.

10. When $x = 3.1$, $5x + 0.5 =$ _____.

11. When $x = 0$, $4x^2 + 5 =$ _____.

12. When $x = 10$, $x^2 - 8x + 11 =$ _____.

13. When $x = 2\frac{1}{2}$, $6x + 3 =$ _____.

Evaluate the perimeter when $x = 3$.

14. 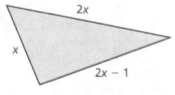 $P =$ _____

15. $P =$ _____

16. **CARDINAL** The weight of the cardinal (in ounces) is $0.6x + 11$ after its eats x ounces of bird seed. How much does it weigh after it eats 2 ounces of bird seed? _____

REVIEW: Writing Expressions and Equations

Key Concept and Vocabulary

Phrase: Two more than a number

Expression: $2 + n$

Sentence: Two more than a number is equal to six.

Equation: $2 + n = 6$

Visual Model

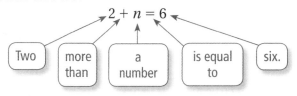

$$2 + n = 6$$

| Two | more than | a number | is equal to | six. |

Skill Examples

1. Five times a number: $5n$

2. Six less than three times a number: $3n - 6$

3. The sum of a number and one: $n + 1$

4. A number divided by three: $n \div 3$

Application Example

5. Write an equation for the following.
   "The price of $15 is the wholesale cost plus a markup of fifty percent."

   Let C be the wholesale cost.
   50% of C is $0.5C$.

   ∴ An equation is $15 = C + 0.5C$.

PRACTICE MAKES *PURR*-FECT™

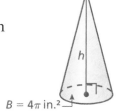

Check your answers at BigIdeasMath.com.

Write the verbal phrase as a mathematical expression.

6. The product of a number and two

   _____

7. 10 subtracted from a number

   _____

8. 19 less than twice a number

   _____

9. The sum of a number and three, divided by four

   _____

10. Five times the sum of a number and two

    _____

11. Seven less than four times a number

    _____

Write the sentence as an equation.

12. Three times a number equals nine.

    _____

13. The difference of a number and nine is four.

    _____

14. Twelve divided by a number is four.

    _____

15. The sum of a number and seven is eighteen.

    _____

16. The volume of a cone is one-third the area of the base times the height. A cone has a volume of 20π cubic inches. Write an equation that can be used to solve for the height of the cone.

    _____

h

$B = 4\pi \text{ in.}^2$

REVIEW: Simplifyng Expressions

Name _____

Key Concept and Vocabulary

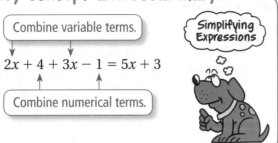

Combine variable terms.

$$2x + 4 + 3x - 1 = 5x + 3$$

Combine numerical terms.

Visual Model

Algebra Tiles

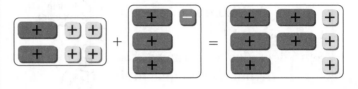

Skill Examples

1. $2x + 5x = 7x$

2. $1 + n + 4 = n + 5$

3. $(2x + 3) - (x + 2) = x + 1$

4. $2(y - 1) + 3(y + 2) = 5y + 4$

Application Example

5. The original cost of a shirt is x dollars. The shirt is on sale for 30% off. Write a simplifed expression for the sale cost.

$$x - 0.3x = 0.7x$$

The sale cost is $0.7x$.

PRACTICE MAKES PURR-FECT™

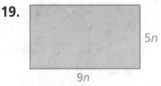

Check your answers at BigIdeasMath.com.

Simplify the expression. (Remove parentheses and combine like terms.)

6. $4x + 6x = $ _____

7. $3n + 5 - 2n = $ _____

8. $9x + 3 - 6x - 2 = $ _____

9. $3(x + 2) = $ _____

10. $7m - 2m + 5m = $ _____

11. $2 - (x + 1) = $ _____

12. $(3x + 6) - x = $ _____

13. $5 - (1 - n) = $ _____

14. $(x + 6) - (x + 6) = $ _____

15. $(4x - 2) + 3(x + 1) = $ _____

16. $(5x + 4) - 2(x + 1) = $ _____

17. $5(x + 2) - 2(x + 2) = $ _____

Write a simplified expression for the perimeter of the rectangle or triangle.

18.

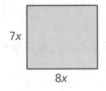

$7x$

$8x$

Perimeter = _____

19.

$5n$

$9n$

Perimeter = _____

20.

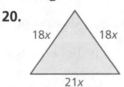

$18x$ $18x$

$21x$

Perimeter = _____

21. The original cost of a cell phone is x dollars. The phone is on sale for 35% off. Write a simplified expression for the sale cost. _____

REVIEW: Writing and Graphing Inequalities

Name _____

Key Concept and Vocabulary

$x > 2$: All numbers greater than 2

$x \geq 2$: All numbers greater than or equal to 2

$x < 2$: All numbers less than 2

$x \leq 2$: All numbers less than or equal to 2

Visual Model

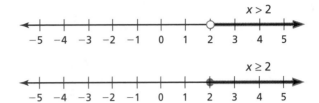

Skill Examples

1. $x > 0$: All positive numbers

2. $x \geq 0$: All nonnegative numbers

3. $x < 0$: All negative numbers

4. $x \leq 0$: All nonpositive numbers

Application Example

5. A sign at a clothing store reads "Savings up to 70%." Let S represent the percent of savings. Write an inequality to describe S.

   S can be equal to 70%.

   Or S can be less than 70%.

   ⋮ An inequality is $S \leq 70\%$.

PRACTICE MAKES *PURR*-FECT™

Check your answers at BigIdeasMath.com.

Write an inequality for the statement.

6. All numbers that are less than 24

   _____

7. All numbers that are at most 3

   _____

8. All numbers greater than 10

   _____

9. All numbers that are no more than 5

   _____

10. All numbers that are at least 11

    _____

11. All numbers less than or equal to 8

    _____

Graph the inequality.

12. $x > -1$

13. $x < 4$

14. $x \leq 3$

15. $x \geq 0$

16. A sign at a shoe store reads "Savings up to 60%." Let P represent the percent of savings. Write an inequality to describe P.

    _____

$45

$65

Shoe Sale
Savings
up to 60%

REVIEW: Ratios

Name _____

Key Concept and Vocabulary

The ratio of 3 red buttons to 2 blue buttons can be written in three ways:

$$\frac{3}{2}, \quad 3 \text{ to } 2, \quad \text{or} \quad 3:2$$

Visual Model

← 3 red buttons

← 2 blue buttons

Skill Examples

1. Ratio of blue buttons to red buttons: $\frac{2}{3}$

2. Ratio of blue buttons to all buttons: $\frac{2}{5}$

3. Ratio of red buttons to all buttons: $\frac{3}{5}$

Application Example

4. Write the ratio of basketballs to soccer balls in three ways.

   There are 4 basketballs.
   There are 5 soccer balls.

   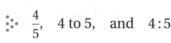 $\frac{4}{5}$,   4 to 5,   and   4 : 5

PRACTICE MAKES PURR-FECT™

Check your answers at BigIdeasMath.com.

Write the *simplified* ratio of green objects to blue objects in three ways.

5.

   _____

6.

   _____

7.

   _____

8.

   _____

Write the simplified ratio of blue objects to *all* objects in three ways.

9. Frogs in Exercise 5

   _____

10. Balloons in Exercise 6

   _____

11. Cars in Exericise 7

   _____

12. Flowers in Exercise 8

   _____

13. **CLASS RATIO** The ratio of boys to girls in a class is 5 to 4. There are 12 girls in the class. How many boys are in the class? _____

REVIEW: Rates

Name _____

Key Concept and Vocabulary

You pay $12 for 4 hot dogs.

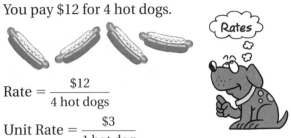

$$\text{Rate} = \frac{\$12}{4 \text{ hot dogs}}$$

$$\text{Unit Rate} = \frac{\$3}{1 \text{ hot dog}}$$

Visual Model

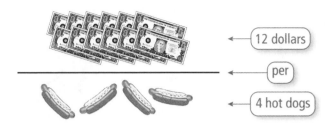

← 12 dollars

← per

← 4 hot dogs

Skill Examples

1. You drive 100 miles in 2 hours.
   Your unit rate is 50 miles per hour.

2. You earn $40 in 5 hours.
   Your unit rate is $8 per hour.

3. You save $240 in 6 months.
   Your unit rate is $40 per month.

Application Example

4. Janice was 44 inches tall when she was 8 years old. She was 52 inches tall when she was 12 years old. What was her unit rate?

   She grew 8 inches in 4 years: $\frac{8}{4} = \frac{2}{1}$.

   Her unit rate is 2 inches per year.

PRACTICE MAKES PURR-FECT™

Check your answers at BigIdeasMath.com.

Write the unit rate in words and as a fraction for each situation.

5. You fly 2000 miles in 4 hours.

   _____   _____
   Words   Fraction

6. You pay 15 dollars for 3 pizzas.

   _____   _____
   Words   Fraction

7. You pay $4 sales tax on a $50 purchase. _____   _____
   Words   Fraction

8. You earn $25 for mowing 5 lawns.

   _____   _____
   Words   Fraction

Circle the name of the person with the greater unit rate.

9. Maria saves $50 in 4 months.
   Ralph saves $60 in 5 months.

10. John rides his bicycle 36 miles in 3 hours.
    Randy rides his bicycle 30 miles in 2.5 hours.

11. Kim earns $400 for working 40 hours.
    Sam earns $540 for working 45 hours.

12. Arlene scores 450 points on 5 tests.
    Jolene scores 180 points on 2 tests.

Convert the unit rate.

13. $\dfrac{60 \text{ miles}}{1 \text{ hour}} = \dfrac{\boxed{} \text{ feet}}{1 \text{ second}}$

14. $\dfrac{2 \text{ gallons}}{1 \text{ hour}} = \dfrac{\boxed{} \text{ cups}}{1 \text{ minute}}$

REVIEW: Proportions

Name _____

Key Concept and Vocabulary

Proportion: "2 is to 3 as 4 is to 6."

$$\frac{2}{3} = \frac{4}{6}$$

$2 \cdot 6 = 3 \cdot 4$ ◄— Cross products are equal.

Proportions

Visual Model

The ratio "2 to 3" is equal to the ratio "4 to 6."

Skill Examples

1. $\dfrac{3}{5} = \dfrac{12}{20}$ is a proportion because the cross products are equal.

2. $\dfrac{1}{7} = \dfrac{7}{48}$ is *not* a proportion because the cross products are not equal.

3. $\dfrac{10}{2} = \dfrac{5}{1}$ is a proportion because the cross products are equal.

Application Example

4. You spend $5 for 3 tennis balls. Your friend spends $6.25 for 4 tennis balls. Are the two rates proportional?

$$\frac{\$5}{3 \text{ balls}} \overset{?}{=} \frac{\$6.25}{4 \text{ balls}} \qquad 5(4) \neq 3(6.25)$$

∴ The rates are *not* proportional.

PRACTICE MAKES PURR-FECT™

Check your answers at BigIdeasMath.com.

Decide whether the statement is a proportion.

5. $\dfrac{3}{7} = \dfrac{6}{14}$ _____

6. $\dfrac{1}{4} = \dfrac{4}{1}$ _____

7. $\dfrac{3}{2} = \dfrac{9}{4}$ _____

8. $\dfrac{1.25}{3} = \dfrac{5}{12}$ _____

9. $\dfrac{6}{18} = \dfrac{120}{360}$ _____

10. $\dfrac{4}{5} = \dfrac{4+4}{5+5}$ _____

Complete the proportion.

11. $\dfrac{2}{5} = \dfrac{\square}{10}$

12. $\dfrac{1}{6} = \dfrac{4}{\square}$

13. $\dfrac{3}{\square} = \dfrac{9}{24}$

Write the proportion that compares the circumference to the radii of the two circles.

14.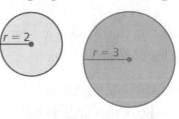

_____

15.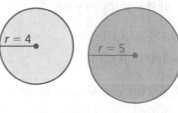

_____

16. **COMPARING RATES** You spend $20 for 5 T-shirts. Your friend spends $15 for 3 T-shirts. Are the two rates proportional? _____

REVIEW: Simple Interest

Name _____

Key Concept and Vocabulary

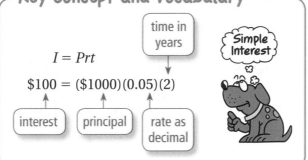

$I = Prt$

$\$100 = (\$1000)(0.05)(2)$

interest   principal   rate as decimal   time in years

Simple Interest

Visual Model

1 month	3 months	4 months
$t = \dfrac{1}{12}$	$t = \dfrac{1}{4}$	$t = \dfrac{1}{3}$

6 months	1 year	2 years
$t = \dfrac{1}{2}$	$t = 1$	$t = 2$

Skill Examples

1. $P = \$200$, $r = 0.10$, $t = 4$ years
   $I = (200)(0.10)(4) = \$80$

2. $P = \$250$, $r = 0.04$, $t = 0.5$ year
   $I = (250)(0.04)(0.5) = \$5$

3. $P = \$2000$, $r = 0.05$, $t = 20$ years
   $I = (2000)(0.05)(20) = \$2000$

Application Example

4. You deposited $500 in a savings account for 10 years. The account paid 6% simple interest. How much interest did you earn?

   $P = \$500$, $r = 0.06$, $t = 10$ years
   $I = (500)(0.06)(10) = \$300$

   ❖ You earned $300 in interest.

PRACTICE MAKES *PURR*-FECT™

Check your answers at BigIdeasMath.com.

Find the simple interest.

5. Principal: $400, Rate: 5%, Time: 3 years

   _____

6. Principal: $100, Rate: 3%, Time: 6 months

   _____

7. Principal: $1000, Rate: 2%, Time: 4 months

   _____

8. Principal: $250, Rate: 10%, Time: 6 months

   _____

9. Principal: $500, Rate: 8%, Time: 9 months

   _____

10. Principal: $600, Rate: 1%, Time: 8 years

   _____

In which savings account do you earn more simple interest?

11. **a.** Deposit $200 at 6% for 3 years.

    b. Deposit $200 at 8% for 18 months.

    _____

12. **a.** Deposit $1000 at 4% for 5 years.

    b. Deposit $1000 at 5% for 4 years.

    _____

13. **SAVINGS** You deposited $600 in a savings account for 5 years. The account paid 4% simple interest. How much interest did you earn? _____

14. **LOAN** You borrowed $1000 for 2 years. You are charged 5% simple interest. How much interest do you owe? _____

REVIEW: Linear Patterns

Name _____

Key Concept and Vocabulary

Equation: $y = 2x + 3$

Table:

x	0	1	2	3	4	5
y	3	5	7	9	11	13

Words: Each time x increases by 1, y increases by 2.

Linear Patterns

Visual Model

Moving to the right, each bar increases by 2 units.

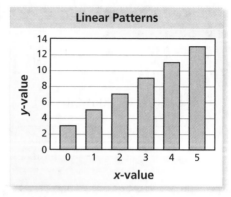

Skill Example

1. **Equation:** $y = 15 - 3x$

   Table:

x	0	1	2	3	4	5
y	15	12	9	6	3	0

   Words: Each time x increases by 1, y *decreases* by 3.

Application Example

2. The equation $P = 5t$ describes how much pay P you earn for working t hours. Make a table and describe the pattern.

t	1	2	3	4	5	6
P	5	10	15	20	25	30

   You get paid $5 an hour.

PRACTICE MAKES *PURR-FECT*™

Check your answers at BigIdeasMath.com.

Complete the table. Then describe the pattern.

3. $y = x + 7$

x	0	1	2	3	4	5
y						

   _____
   _____

4. $y = 9 - x$

x	0	1	2	3	4	5
y						

   _____
   _____

5. $y = 4x + 5$

x	0	1	2	3	4	5
y						

   _____
   _____

6. $y = 90 - 6x$

x	0	1	2	3	4	5
y						

   _____
   _____

Write an equation for the pattern.

7.

x	0	1	2	3	4	5
y	5	14	23	32	41	50

_____

8.

x	0	1	2	3	4	5
y	50	40	30	20	10	0

_____

9. **HOURLY PAY** The equation $P = 7t$ describes how much pay P you earn for working t hours. Describe the pattern. _____

REVIEW: Function Rules

Key Concept and Vocabulary

Function Rule: $y = 2x + 4$

output — input

Words: Double the value of x and add 4 to get the value of y.

Visual Model

You can see how x and y compare by making an Input-Output table.

Function Rule: $y = 2x + 4$

Input, x	0	1	2	3	4	5
Output, y	4	6	8	10	12	14

Skill Example

1. **Equation:** $y = 20 - 4x$

   Table:

Input, x	0	1	2	3	4	5
Output, y	20	16	12	8	4	0

   Words: Multiply x by 4 and subtract from 20 to get the value of y.

Application Example

2. The equation $F = \frac{9}{5}C + 32$ describes how the Fahrenheit and Celsius scales relate. Describe this in words.

Input, C	0	5	10	15	20	25
Output, F	32	41	50	59	68	77

   Multiply C by $\frac{9}{5}$ and add 32 to get F.

PRACTICE MAKES PURR-FECT™

Check your answers at BigIdeasMath.com.

Complete the table. Then describe the pattern.

3. $y = 2x + 6$

Input, x	0	1	2	3	4	5
Output, y						

_____
_____

4. $y = 16 - 2x$

Input, x	0	1	2	3	4	5
Output, y						

_____
_____

5. $y = 3x + 7$

Input, x	0	1	2	3	4	5
Output, y						

_____
_____

6. $y = 65 - 10x$

Input, x	0	1	2	3	4	5
Output, y						

_____
_____

UNIT CONVERSION **Complete the table and describe the function rule in words.**

7. Inches to Centimeters: $C = 2.54I$

Input, I	0	1	2	3	4	5
Output, C						

8. Miles to Kilometers: $K = 1.6M$

Input, M	0	1	2	3	4	5
Output, K						

_____   _____

REVIEW: Direct Variation

Name _____

Key Concept and Vocabulary

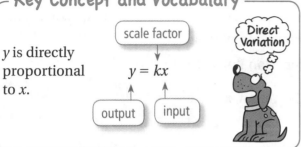

y is directly proportional to x.

scale factor

$y = kx$

output   input

Direct Variation

Visual Model

For positive values of x and y, as x increases, y increases.

$$y = \frac{1}{2}x$$

through origin

Skill Example

1. **Equation:** $y = 2x$

   Table:

x	0	1	2	3	4	5
y	0	2	4	6	8	10

   Words: y is twice the value of x.

Application Example

2. The amount y of gasoline a car uses is $\frac{1}{20}$ times the number x of miles it travels. Make a table to show this relationship.

x	0	20	40	60	80	100
y	0	1	2	3	4	5

   ⋮ y is directly proportional to x.

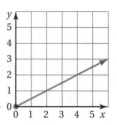

PRACTICE MAKES PURR-FECT™

Check your answers at BigIdeasMath.com.

Complete the table. Then sketch the graph.

3. $y = 1.5x$

x	y
0	
1	
2	
3	
4	

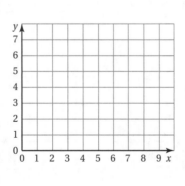

4. $y = \frac{2}{3}x$

x	y
0	
1	
2	
3	
4	

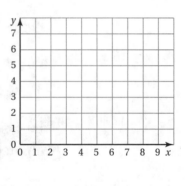

WRITING AN EQUATION Write a direct variation equation for the table.

5.

x	0	1	2	3	4
y	0	3	6	9	12

_____

6.

x	0	1	2	3	4
y	0	0.4	0.8	1.2	1.6

_____

7. **WALRUS** The amount y that a walrus eats is directly proportional to its weight x. A 4000 pound walrus eats 20 pounds each day. How much does a 2000 pound walrus eat each day? _____

REVIEW: Graphs of Equations

Key Concept and Vocabulary

Equation: $y = 3 - \dfrac{3}{4}x$

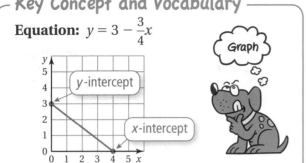

Visual Model

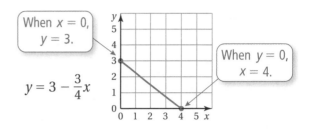

When $x = 0$, $y = 3$.

$y = 3 - \dfrac{3}{4}x$

When $y = 0$, $x = 4$.

Skill Example

1. Equation: $y = 3 - \dfrac{3}{4}x$

Table:

x	0	1	2	3	4	5
y	3	$\dfrac{9}{4}$	$\dfrac{3}{2}$	$\dfrac{3}{4}$	0	$-\dfrac{3}{4}$

Application Example

2. A parachutist's height h (in feet) is given by $h = 450 - 15t$, where t is the time in seconds. When does the parachutist land?

t	0	5	10	15	20	25	30
h	450	375	300	225	150	75	0

∴ After 30 seconds, the height is 0 feet.

PRACTICE MAKES *PURR*-FECT™

Check your answers at BigIdeasMath.com.

Complete the table. Then sketch the graph.

3. $y = 4 - x$

x	y
0	
1	
2	
3	
4	

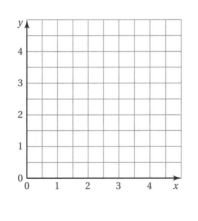

4. $y = \dfrac{1}{2}x + 2$

x	y
0	
1	
2	
3	
4	

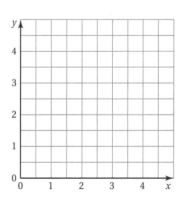

Find the x-intercept and y-intercept of the graph of the equation.

5. $y = 5 - x$ x-intercept = _____

                  y-intercept = _____

6. $y = 5 - \dfrac{1}{2}x$ x-intercept = _____

                   y-intercept = _____

7. PARACHUTE FALL A parachutist's height h (in feet) is given by $h = 1000 - 20t$, where t is the time in seconds. When does the parachutist land?

_____

REVIEW: Variables

Name _____

Key Concept and Vocabulary

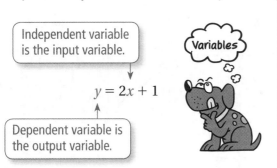

Independent variable is the input variable.

$y = 2x + 1$

Dependent variable is the output variable.

Variables

Visual Model

Independent Variable	Expression	Dependent Variable
x	$2x + 1$	y
1	$2(1) + 1$	3
2	$2(2) + 1$	5
3	$2(3) + 1$	7

Skill Examples

1. In $y = 3x - 2$, x is the independent variable and y is the dependent variable.

2. In $C = 2\pi r$, r is the independent variable and C is the dependent variable.

3. In $A = \ell w$, ℓ and w are the independent variables and A is the dependent variable.

Application Example

4. Your income i is calculated from the total time t worked. Identify the independent variable and the dependent variable.

   ⋮ Total time t is the independent variable and your income i is the dependent variable.

PRACTICE MAKES PURR-FECT™

Check your answers at BigIdeasMath.com.

Identify the independent variable(s) and the dependent variable.

5. $y = 6x + 1$ _____

6. $A = \frac{1}{2}bh$ _____

7. $A = \pi r^2$ _____

8. $m = 15 - n$ _____

9. $V = \ell wh$ _____

10. $P = 2\ell + 2w$ _____

11.

Hours Studying, h	Test Score, s
2	72%
3	80%
5	91%
7	98%

_____

12.

Number of CDs, n	Total Cost, c
1	$9.99
2	$19.98
3	$29.97
4	$39.96

_____

13. **DISTANCE** To find the distance d traveled, you multiply the rate r by the time t. Identify the independent variables and the dependent variable.

_____

REVIEW: Tree Diagrams

Name _____

Key Concept and Vocabulary

Flip a coin
2 times.
4 possible
outcomes:
HH, HT, TH, TT

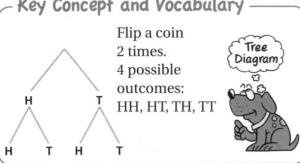

Visual Model

HH   HT   TH   TT

Skill Example

1.

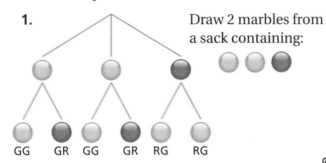

GG   GR   GG   GR   RG   RG

Draw 2 marbles from
a sack containing:

Application Example

2. You are drawing 2 marbles from a sack that
contains . In how many ways can
you draw 2 green marbles?

There are 2 GG's in the tree diagram.

∴ There are 2 ways to draw 2 green marbles.

PRACTICE MAKES PURR-FECT™

Check your answers at BigIdeasMath.com.

Draw a tree diagram to show all the outcomes.

3. Flip a coin 3 times.

4. Draw 2 marbles from a sack with .

5. You flip a coin 3 times. In how many ways
can you get 2 heads and 1 tail? _____

6. You draw 2 marbles from a sack with .
In how many ways can you draw
2 green marbles? _____

7. **CARDS** You draw 2 cards from the hand at the right.
In how many ways can you end up with a sum of 5?
(For instance, A + 4 = 5.) _____

_____

REVIEW: Counting Principle

Key Concept and Vocabulary

Event 1 can occur in *m* ways.
Event 2 can occur in *n* ways.

 Counting Principle

Event 1 followed by Event 2 can occur in $m \times n$ ways.

Multiply.

Visual Model

4 flavor choices for 1st scoop

4 flavor choices for 2nd scoop

$4 \times 4 = 16$ "two-scoop" cones

Skill Example

1. Event 1 can occur in 6 ways.
   Event 2 can occur in 3 ways.

   Event 1 followed by Event 2 can occur in

   $6 \times 3 = 18$ ways.

Application Example

2. How many outfits can you make using 3 T-shirts and 4 pairs of jeans?

   $3 \times 4 = 12$ outfits

   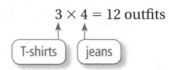
   T-shirts   jeans

   You can make 12 different outfits.

PRACTICE MAKES *PURR*-FECT™

Check your answers at BigIdeasMath.com.

Find the number of ways that Event 1 can occur followed by Event 2.

3. Event 1 can occur in 5 ways.
   Event 2 can occur in 6 ways.

   _____

4. Event 1 can occur in 10 ways.
   Event 2 can occur in 3 ways.

   _____

5. Event 1 can occur in 11 ways.
   Event 2 can occur in 11 ways.

   _____

6. Event 1 can occur in 14 ways.
   Event 2 can occur in 4 ways.

   _____

Find the number of ways that Event 1 can occur followed by Event 2, followed by Event 3.

7. Event 1 can occur in 2 ways.
   Event 2 can occur in 4 ways.
   Event 3 can occur in 5 ways.

   _____

8. Event 1 can occur in 8 ways.
   Event 2 can occur in 7 ways.
   Event 3 can occur in 6 ways.

   _____

9. **OUTFITS** How many different outfits can you make using the T-shirts and jeans shown at the right? _____

10. **OUTFITS** How many of the outfits have the gray jeans? _____

REVIEW: Permutations

Name _____

Key Concept and Vocabulary

4 marbles can be arranged in $4 \cdot 3 \cdot 2 \cdot 1 = 24$ orders.

$4! = 4 \cdot 3 \cdot 2 \cdot 1$

$\qquad = 24$

4 factorial

Permutation

Visual Model

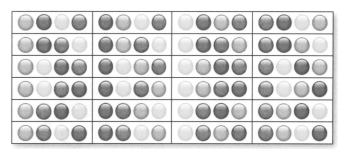

Skill Examples

1. $1! = 1$

2. $2! = 2 \cdot 1 = 2$

3. $5! = 5 \cdot 4 \cdot 3 \cdot 2 \cdot 1 = 120$

4. $6! = 6 \cdot 5 \cdot 4 \cdot 3 \cdot 2 \cdot 1 = 720$

5. $8! = 40,320$

Application Example

6. In how many different orders can 5 people stand in line?

5 factorial

$5! = 5 \cdot 4 \cdot 3 \cdot 2 \cdot 1 = 120$

⋮ They can stand in 120 different orders.

PRACTICE MAKES *PURR*-FECT™

Check your answers at BigIdeasMath.com.

Evaluate the factorial.

7. $3! = $ _____

8. $4! = $ _____

9. $7! = $ _____

10. **MARBLES** Draw all the different ways that you can order 3 marbles.

11. **DIGITS** Write all the numbers you can form with the digits 1, 2, 3, and 4. *(No repeats.)*

$1, 2, 3, 4$

12. **CALLING FRIENDS** You are calling six friends to invite them to a party. In how many different orders can you call them? _____

13. **FINISHING A RACE** Four runners are in a race. In how many different orders can they cross the finish line? *(No ties.)* _____

14. **DVDs ON A SHELF** You have 8 DVDs. In how many different ways can you order them on a shelf? _____

REVIEW: Combinations

Name _____

Key Concept and Vocabulary

You can choose 2 out of 4 marbles

in 6 ways (order does not matter).

Combination

Visual Model

Be careful not to double count ways. Order does not matter for combinations.

Skill Example

1. You can choose 3 out of 4 marbles

   in 4 ways (order does not matter).

Application Example

2. How many 2-person committees can you form from 5 people?

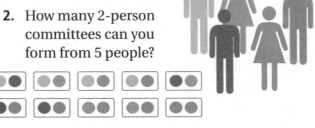

   You can form 10 different committees.

PRACTICE MAKES PURR-FECT™

Check your answers at BigIdeasMath.com.

3. **FIGURES** Draw all the ways that you can choose 2 figures out of 3 figures. ■ ● ▲

4. **COMMITTEES** How many 3-person committees can you form from 5 people? *(Draw a sketch for each committee.)* _____   ⓵ ⓶ ⓷ ⓸ ⓹

5. **PAIRS OF SOCKS** How many pairs of socks can you make from 7 identical socks? *(Draw a sketch for each pair.)* _____   ⓵ ⓶ ⓷ ⓸ ⓹ ⓺ ⓻

6. **RIDING IN AN SUV** Eight people want to ride in an SUV that can only hold 7 people. How many groups of 7 people can be chosen from the 8 people? Explain.

   _____

   _____

   _____

REVIEW: Sample Space

Name _____

Key Concept and Vocabulary

The set of all outcomes of an experiment is called the **sample space**.

The sum of the probabilities of all outcomes in a sample space is 1.

Outcomes

Visual Model

A hat contains 3 tiles with the letters P, R, and O.

Experiment: Draw a tile.

Sample Space: P   R   O

Probabilities: $\frac{1}{3}$ $\frac{1}{3}$ $\frac{1}{3}$

Sum of Probabilities: $\frac{1}{3} + \frac{1}{3} + \frac{1}{3} = 1$

Skill Examples

1. You flip a coin. The sample space of the experiment is Heads (H), Tails (T).

2. You roll a number cube. The sample space of the experiment is 1, 2, 3, 4, 5, 6.

3. You flip a coin and roll a number cube. The sample space of the experiment is H1, H2, H3, H4, H5, H6, T1, T2, T3, T4, T5, T6.

Application Example

4. A referee flips a coin twice. Find the sample space. Show that the sum of the probabilities of all outcomes is 1.

   The sample space is HH, HT, TH, TT.

   The probability of each outcome is $\frac{1}{4}$.

   $\frac{1}{4} + \frac{1}{4} + \frac{1}{4} + \frac{1}{4} = 1$

PRACTICE MAKES *PURR-FECT*™

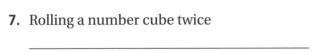

Check your answers at BigIdeasMath.com.

Find the sample space of the experiment.

5. Drawing a marble

   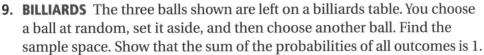

   _____

6. Rolling a cube with letters of the word *sample*

      _____

7. Rolling a number cube twice

   _____
   _____
   _____

8. Flipping a coin and rolling the cube in Exercise 6

   _____
   _____

9. **BILLIARDS** The three balls shown are left on a billiards table. You choose a ball at random, set it aside, and then choose another ball. Find the sample space. Show that the sum of the probabilities of all outcomes is 1.

   _____

   _____

BASIC
SKILLS
HANDBOOK

Rounding Numbers

Name _____

Key Concept and Vocabulary

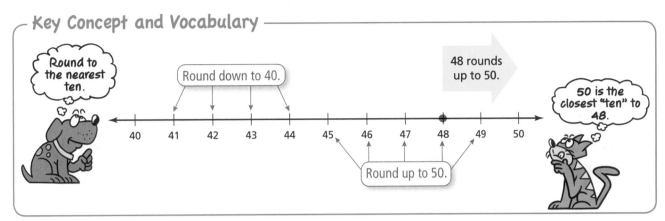

Round to the nearest ten.

Round down to 40.

48 rounds up to 50.

50 is the closest "ten" to 48.

Round up to 50.

PRACTICE MAKES *PURR*-FECT™

Check your answers at BigIdeasMath.com.

Circle the closest "ten." Then write the answer in [ ].

1. ←─┼──┼──●──┼──┼──┼──┼──┼──┼──┼──┼──→
   30 31 32 33 34 35 36 37 38 39 40

   32 rounds to [ ] .

2. ←─┼──┼──┼──┼──┼──┼──┼──┼──┼──●──┼──→
   60 61 62 63 64 65 66 67 68 69 70

   69 rounds to [ ] .

3. ←─┼──┼──┼──┼──┼──┼──┼──●──┼──┼──┼──→
   10 11 12 13 14 15 16 17 18 19 20

   17 rounds to [ ] .

4. ←─┼──●──┼──┼──┼──┼──┼──┼──┼──┼──┼──→
   90 91 92 93 94 95 96 97 98 99 100

   91 rounds to [ ] .

Count the money. Circle the better statement.

5.

   The total is about 40¢.

   The total is about 30¢.

6.

   The total is about 40¢.

   The total is about 30¢.

7. **BIOLOGY** You are counting trout in a stream. To the *nearest ten*, [ ] trout about how many are there?

Adding and Subtracting

Name _____

Key Concept and Vocabulary

Use counters to add & subtract.

$3 + 2 = 5$

$3 - 2 = 1$

+ means add
− means subtract.

PRACTICE MAKES *PURR*-FECT™

Check your answers at BigIdeasMath.com.

Draw the correct number of ●. Write the answer in ▢.

1. ▢ + ▢ = [ ]

$4 + 2 =$ ▢

2. ▢ − ▢ = [ ]

$4 - 2 =$ ▢

3. ▢ + ▢ = [ ]

$4 + 1 =$ ▢

4. ▢ − ▢ = [ ]

$4 - 1 =$ ▢

Write the problem in ▢.

5. ▢ + ▢ = ▢   ▢ + ▢ = ▢

6. ▢ − ▢ = ▢   ▢ − ▢ = ▢

7. CAR WASH Twelve cars went to the car wash. Eight cars have been washed. How many still need to be washed?

▢ cars

Multiplying

Name _____

Key Concept and Vocabulary

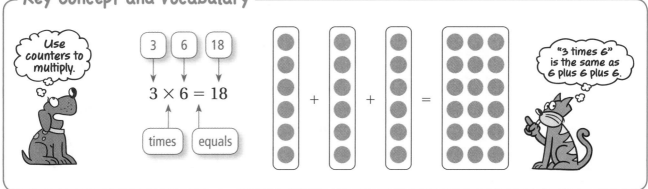

Use counters to multiply.

3   6   18

$3 \times 6 = 18$

times   equals

+   +   =

"3 times 6" is the same as 6 plus 6 plus 6.

PRACTICE MAKES *PURR*-FECT™

Check your answers at BigIdeasMath.com.

Draw the correct number of ●. Write the answer in ▢.

1.

▢ + ▢ + ▢ + ▢ = ●●●●
                    ●●●●
                    ●●●●

$4 \times 3 = $ ▢

2.

● + ● + ● + ● + ● = ▢
●   ●   ●   ●   ●

$5 \times 2 = $ ▢

Write the problem in ▢.

3. ▢ × ▢ = ▢

● + ● + ● + ● + ● = ●●●●●
●   ●   ●   ●   ●   ●●●●●
●   ●   ●   ●   ●   ●●●●●
●   ●   ●   ●   ●   ●●●●●

4. ▢ × ▢ = ▢

● + ● + ● + ● = ●●●●
●   ●   ●   ●   ●●●●

5. TEXT MESSAGES Each cell phone has four text messages. Find the total number of text messages.

▢ text messages

Dividing

Key Concept and Vocabulary

Use counters to divide.

18   3   6

$18 \div 3 = 6$

divided by   equals

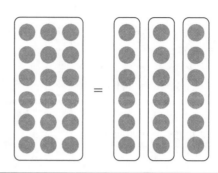

I like it. 18 is equal to 3 groups of 6.

PRACTICE MAKES PURR-FECT™

Check your answers at BigIdeasMath.com.

Draw the correct number of . Write the answer in ▢.

1. [   ] = [●●●] [●●●] [●●●] [●●●] $12 \div 4 =$ ▢

2. [●●●●● ●●●●●] = [ ] [ ] [ ] [ ] [ ] $10 \div 5 =$ ▢

Write the problem in ▢.

3. ▢ ÷ ▢ = ▢

4. ▢ ÷ ▢ = ▢

5. **SHARING** You have twenty quarters to share equally with four people. How many does each person get?

    ▢ quarters

Key Concept and Vocabulary

Count the number of flowers.

1 2 3 5 4 + 6

If you add one more flower you will have 5 + 1 = 6 flowers.

PRACTICE MAKES *PURR*-FECT™

Check your answers at BigIdeasMath.com.

1. Count the number of animals.

[ ] animals

How many animals do you have if you add one more?

[ ] animals

2. Count the number of fish.

[ ] fish

How many fish do you have if you add one more?

[ ] fish

Decide whether the number of cherries in each bunch is the same or different.

3.

Same

Different

4.

Same

Different

Key Concept and Vocabulary

  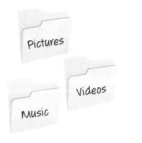 

Count the number of folders.

English Spanish Science Math Pictures Music Videos

Because 4+3=7, there are 7 folders.

4 + 3

PRACTICE MAKES *PURR*-FECT™

Check your answers at BigIdeasMath.com.

1. How many items are in your bookbag if you take away the CD's?

2. The activities that you and your friend are involved in are shown. How many activities do you and your friend do?

You:

Your Friend:

3. Count the number of baseball players.

_____ baseball players

How many baseball players do you have if you add one more?

_____ baseball players

4. Count the number of lizards.

_____ lizards

How many lizards do you have if you take one away?

_____ lizards

Adding and Subtracting Whole Numbers

Name _____

Key Concept and Vocabulary

Remember to carry the tens digit to the next column.

Find 114 + 87.

$$\begin{array}{r} 11 \\ 114 \\ +\ 87 \\ \hline 201 \end{array}$$

The sum is 201.

PRACTICE MAKES *PURR*-FECT™

Check your answers at BigIdeasMath.com.

1. Find 57 + 32.

2. Find 133 + 125.

3. Find 289 + 463.

4. Find 188 − 58.

5. Find 74 − 57.

6. Find 325 − 158.

7. You missed 13 questions out of 80 questions on a test. How many questions did you get correct?

8. You are traveling 111 miles in an airplane from San Diego to Los Angeles. Then you will travel 225 miles from Los Angeles to Las Vegas. What is the total distance of your trip?

9. The table shows the number of miles you biked each day. Find the number of miles you biked for the whole week.

Mon	Tues	Wed	Thurs	Fri
10	8	13	15	7

Factoring

Name _____

Key Concept and Vocabulary

Rectangles can show factors.

$12 = 1 \times 12$

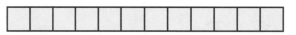

$12 = 2 \times 6$

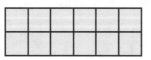

factors

$12 = 3 \times 4$

There are 3 ways to factor 12.

PRACTICE MAKES *PURR*-FECT™

Check your answers at BigIdeasMath.com.

Write the factors shown by the rectangle.

1.

$6 = \boxed{} \times \boxed{}$

2.

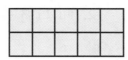

$10 = \boxed{} \times \boxed{}$

3.

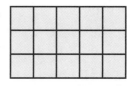

$15 = \boxed{} \times \boxed{}$

4. Factor 8 in 2 ways.

$8 = \boxed{} \times \boxed{}$

$8 = \boxed{} \times \boxed{}$

Draw and shade a rectangle that shows the factors.

5. $30 = 5 \times 6$

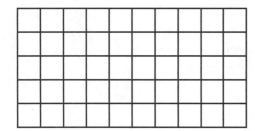

6. $27 = 3 \times 9$

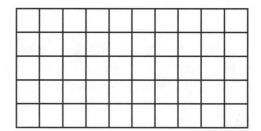

7. STARS AND STRIPES Which American flag shows one way to factor 48? Circle the correct answer.

1959 Flag   1960 Flag

1959 Flag

1960 Flag

Divisibility Tests

Key Concept and Vocabulary

3 divides evenly into 18.

A number is divisible by

2: if its last digit is 0, 2, 4, 6, or 8.

3: if the sum of the digits is divisible by 3.

5: if its last digit is 0 or 5.

10: if its last digit is 0.

I use step counting to help remember.

PRACTICE MAKES *PURR-FECT*™

Check your answers at BigIdeasMath.com.

Circle "Yes" or "No" in each box in the table.

	Number	Is the number divisible by 2?	Is the number divisible by 3?	Is the number divisible by 5?	Is the number divisible by 10?
1.	4	Yes No	Yes No	Yes No	Yes No
2.	5	Yes No	Yes No	Yes No	Yes No
3.	6	Yes No	Yes No	Yes No	Yes No
4.	7	Yes No	Yes No	Yes No	Yes No
5.	8	Yes No	Yes No	Yes No	Yes No
6.	9	Yes No	Yes No	Yes No	Yes No
7.	10	Yes No	Yes No	Yes No	Yes No
8.	11	Yes No	Yes No	Yes No	Yes No
9.	12	Yes No	Yes No	Yes No	Yes No

10. PATTERN Describe the pattern in this column.

_____
_____
_____
_____

11. PATTERN Describe the pattern in this column.

_____
_____
_____
_____
_____

Prime Numbers

Name _____

Key Concept and Vocabulary

Primes must be 2 or more.

A number is **prime** if you *cannot* factor it into smaller numbers.

1	
2	**2 is prime.**
3	**3 is prime.**
4 = 2 × 2	
5	**5 is prime.**

6 = 2 × 3	
7	**7 is prime.**
8 = 2 × 4	
9 = 3 × 3	
10 = 2 × 5	

Remember, you cannot factor primes.

PRACTICE MAKES *PURR*-FECT™

Check your answers at BigIdeasMath.com.

1. **DOT-TO-DOT** Draw the dot-to-dot. Circle each **prime** number.

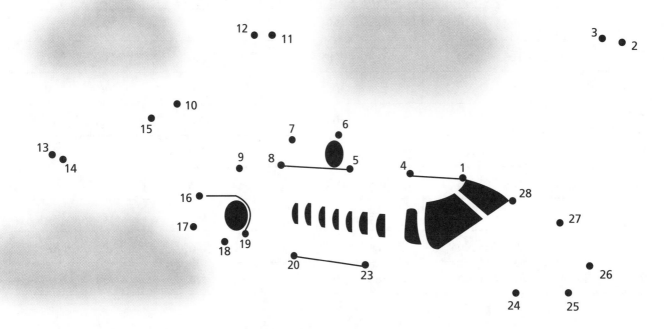

2. What is this picture? _____

3. How many of the numbers from 1 to 28 are prime?

_____

Key Concept and Vocabulary

Multiples form a pattern.

Multiples of 3

1	2	③	4	5	⑥	7	8	⑨
10	11	⑫	13	14	⑮	16	17	⑱
19	20	㉑	22	23	㉔	25	26	㉗
28	29	㉚	31	32	㉝	34	35	㊱

Finding multiples is like step counting.

PRACTICE MAKES *PURR*-FECT™

Check your answers at BigIdeasMath.com.

1. Circle the numbers that are multiples of 2.

1	2	3	4	5	6	7	8	9	10
11	12	13	14	15	16	17	18	19	20
21	22	23	24	25	26	27	28	29	30
31	32	33	34	35	36	37	38	39	40

2. Circle the numbers that are multiples of 5.

1	2	3	4	5	6	7	8	9	10
11	12	13	14	15	16	17	18	19	20
21	22	23	24	25	26	27	28	29	30
31	32	33	34	35	36	37	38	39	40

3. Circle the numbers that are multiples of 2 *and* 5.

1	2	3	4	5	6	7	8	9	10
11	12	13	14	15	16	17	18	19	20
21	22	23	24	25	26	27	28	29	30
31	32	33	34	35	36	37	38	39	40

4. HORSES In a group of horses, the total number of horse hooves is a multiple of _____ .

5. BIRDS In a flock of birds, the total number of wings is a multiple of _____ .

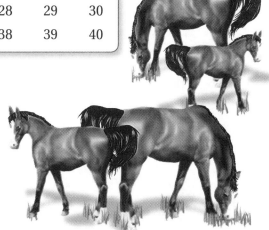

Commutative Property

Name _____

Key Concept and Vocabulary

Add or multiply in any order.

Adding is commutative.

$3 + 4 = 7$
$4 + 3 = 7$

Both orders have the same sum.

Multiplying is commutative.

$3 \times 4 = 12$
$4 \times 3 = 12$

Both orders have the same product.

Order does not matter when you add or multiply.

PRACTICE MAKES *PURR*-FECT™

Check your answers at *BigIdeasMath.com*.

1. Complete the **addition** table.

+	1	2	3	4	5	6	7
1	2	3	4				
2	3	4					
3							
4							
5							
6							
7							

2. Complete the **multiplication** table.

×	1	2	3	4	5	6	7
1	1	2	3				
2	2	4					
3							
4							
5							
6							
7							

3. **PATTERN** Describe the pattern in this table.

_____
_____
_____
_____
_____
_____

4. **PATTERN** Describe the pattern in this table.

_____
_____
_____
_____
_____
_____

Distributive Property

Name _____

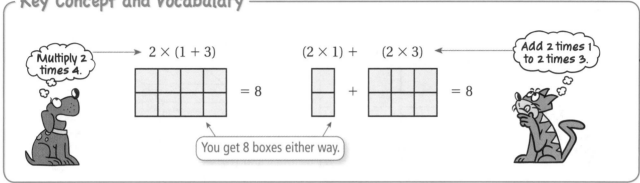

Multiply 2 times 4.

$2 \times (1 + 3)$ = 8

You get 8 boxes either way.

$(2 \times 1) +$ (2×3) = 8

Add 2 times 1 to 2 times 3.

PRACTICE MAKES *PURR*-FECT™

Check your answers at BigIdeasMath.com.

Write the answer in ▢ .

1.  = ▢   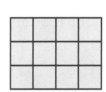 + = ▢

2. = ▢   + = ▢

3. 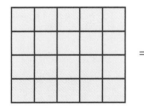 = ▢   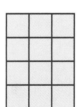 + 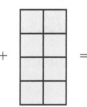 = ▢

4. 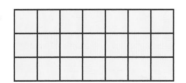 = ▢   + 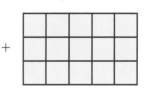 = ▢

Draw lines to match the expressions. Then color the empty boxes to match those above.

5. $2 \times (2 + 3)$ ▢   ▢ $(4 \times 3) + (4 \times 2)$

6. $3 \times (4 + 2)$ ▢   ▢ $(2 \times 2) + (2 \times 3)$

7. $4 \times (3 + 2)$ ▢   ▢ $(3 \times 2) + (3 \times 5)$

8. $3 \times (2 + 5)$ ▢   ▢ $(3 \times 4) + (3 \times 2)$

Exponents

Name _____

Key Concept and Vocabulary

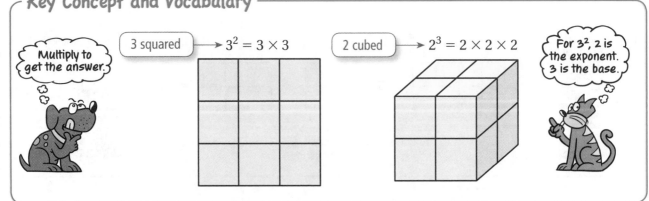

Multiply to get the answer.

3 squared → $3^2 = 3 \times 3$

2 cubed → $2^3 = 2 \times 2 \times 2$

For 3^2, 2 is the exponent. 3 is the base.

PRACTICE MAKES PURR-FECT™

Check your answers at BigIdeasMath.com.

Write the answer in ▢.

1. $4^2 =$ ▢ × ▢

   = ▢

2. $6^2 =$ ▢ × ▢

   = ▢

3. $3^3 =$ ▢ × ▢ × ▢

   = ▢

Draw lines to match the expression with the words.

4. 5^2 ●   ● Four squared

5. 4^2 ●   ● Four cubed

6. 4^3 ●   ● Five cubed

7. 5^3 ●   ● Five squared

Use an exponent to write the area.

8. Area = ▢ square units

9. Area = ▢ square units

10. **FILLING A BOX** How many small boxes can be put in the big box?

    Use an exponent to write your answer.

    ▢ small boxes

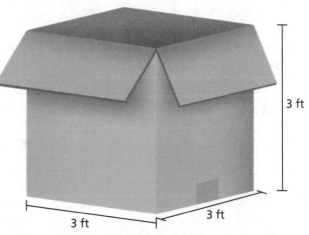

3 ft

1 ft

1 ft   1 ft

3 ft

3 ft

Order of Operations

Name _____

Key Concept and Vocabulary

Order can make a difference.

1st Parentheses → $5 - (1 + 2) = 5 - 3 = 2$

2nd Multiply and divide. → $2 + 3 \times 4 = 2 + 12 = 14$

3rd Add and subtract. → $5 - 3 + 4 = 2 + 4 = 6$

We have to agree on an order.

PRACTICE MAKES *PURR*-FECT™

Check your answers at BigIdeasMath.com.

Write the answer in .

1. $15 - 3 \times 2 =$ ▢

2. $12 + 8 \div 2 =$ ▢

3. $(9 - 4) - 3 =$ ▢

4. $5 \times 4 - 2 =$ ▢

5. $9 - (5 - 4) =$ ▢

6. $16 \div (5 - 3) =$ ▢

7. MAGIC OPERATION SQUARE Use the **numbers** in the boxes to fill in the magic operation square.

4	9	−		+	1	= 6
2	+	▓	×	▓	×	
8		÷		+		= 9
3	−	▓	−	▓	+	
5	6	×		−	7	= 11

‖ ‖ ‖
11 5 12

Comparing Integers

Name _____

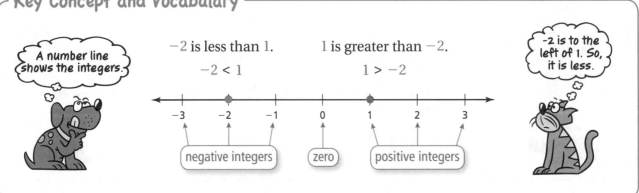
PRACTICE MAKES *PURR*-FECT™

Check your answers at BigIdeasMath.com.

Write the integers in ☐ .

1. ☐ < ☐

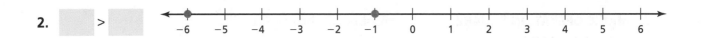

2. ☐ > ☐

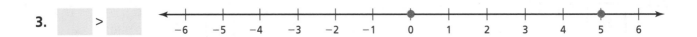

3. ☐ > ☐

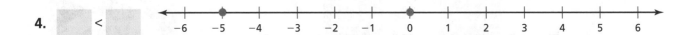

4. ☐ < ☐

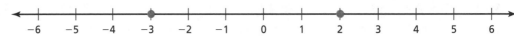

5. **TEMPERATURE** What is the temperature in Fairbanks?

   ☐ degrees

6. **TEMPERATURE** What is the temperature in Anchorage?

   ☐ degrees

7. **TEMPERATURE** Circle the colder temperature.

   Fairbanks   Anchorage

Fairbanks   Anchorage

Coordinate Plane

Name _____

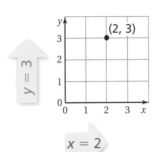

PRACTICE MAKES *PURR*-FECT™

Check your answers at BigIdeasMath.com.

Plot the points. Then draw the dot-to-dot.

1. (1, 11)   **2.** (3, 11)   **3.** (5, 4)   **4.** (8, 11)   **5.** (11, 4)   **6.** (13, 11)

7. (15, 11)   **8.** (12, 1)   **9.** (10, 1)   **10.** (8, 6)   **11.** (6, 1)   **12.** (4, 1)

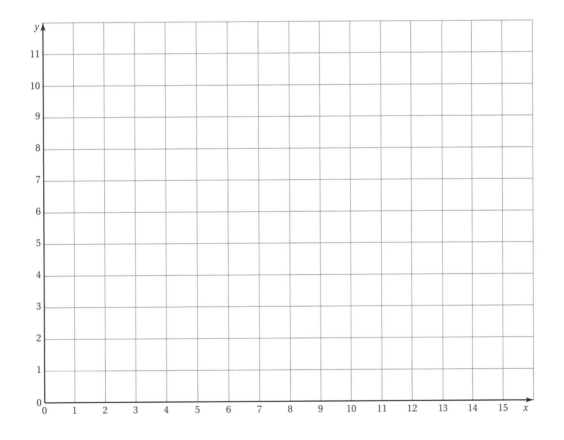

13. ALPHABET What letter of the alphabet did you draw?

Adding Integers

Key Concept and Vocabulary

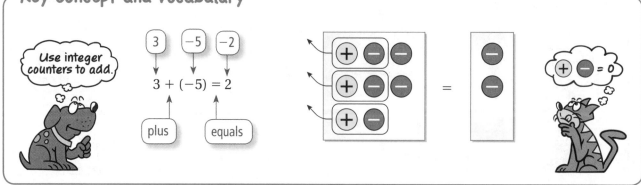

Use integer counters to add.

$$3 + (-5) = 2$$

plus   equals

PRACTICE MAKES PURR-FECT™

Check your answers at BigIdeasMath.com.

Draw the integer counters. Write the integers in ▢ .

1.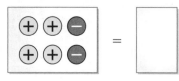

   ☐ + ☐ = ☐

2.

   ☐ + ☐ = ☐

3.

   ☐ + ☐ = ☐

4.

   ☐ + ☐ = ☐

5. **TEMPERATURE** The temperature went up 6 degrees. What is the new temperature?

   ☐ degrees

6. **TEMPERATURE** Write the addition problem shown by the thermometer.

   ☐ + ☐ = ☐

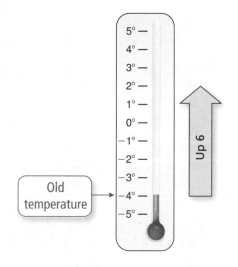

Old temperature

Up 6

Multiplying Integers

Name _____

PRACTICE MAKES PURR-FECT™

Check your answers at BigIdeasMath.com.

Draw the integer counters. Write the problem in [ ] **.**

1. 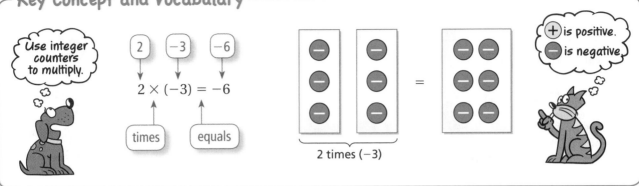 = [_____]   [ ] × [ ] = [ ]

2. = [_____]   [ ] × [ ] = [ ]

3. = [_____]   [ ] × [ ] = [ ]

4. = [_____]   [ ] × [ ] = [ ]

5. **BUSINESS** Your business lost ten dollars (−$10) each day for 4 days. How much did you lose altogether?

    [_____] × [_____] = [_____] dollars

Related Sets

Key Concept and Vocabulary

A table can help describe related sets of numbers.

Set A is one less than Set B, or Set B is one more than Set A.

Set A	1	3	6	7
	+1 ↓↑ −1	+1 ↓↑ −1	+1 ↓↑ −1	+1 ↓↑ −1
Set B	2	4	7	8

PRACTICE MAKES *PURR*-FECT™

Check your answers at BigIdeasMath.com.

Describe the relationship between Set A and Set B.

1.

Set A	1	2	3	4
Set B	2	3	4	5

2.

Set A	1	2	3	4
Set B	0	1	2	3

3.

Set A	4	6	7	9
Set B	3	5	6	8

4.

Set A	2	3	5	8
Set B	3	4	6	9

5.

Set A	6	7	10	13
Set B	5	6	9	12

6.

Set A	8	11	14	17
Set B	9	12	15	18

7.

Set A	−8	−6	−3	−1
Set B	−7	−5	−2	0

8.

Set A	−5	−4	1	6
Set B	−6	−5	0	5

9. TAXI CAB The table shows the cost for riding in a taxi cab. Describe the relationship between the two sets of numbers.

Number of Minutes	Cost
3	$4
5	$6
6	$7
8	$9

Equivalent Fractions

Name _____

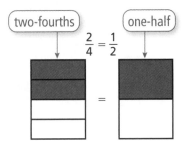
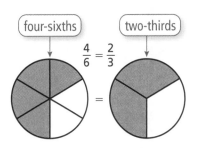

PRACTICE MAKES *PURR*-FECT™

Check your answers at BigIdeasMath.com.

Write the equivalent fractions in ▢ .

1.
 = ▢▢ = ▢

2.
 = ▢▢ = ▢

3.
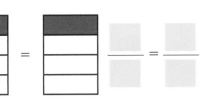 = ▢▢ = ▢

4.
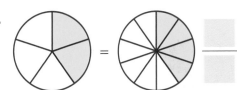 = ▢▢ = ▢

5.
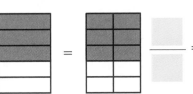 = ▢▢ = ▢

6.
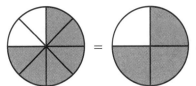 = ▢▢ = ▢

7. **PIZZA** You ate two pieces of the pizza.
   Circle *all* statements that are true.

   I ate one-fourth of the pizza.

   I ate two-sixths of the pizza.

   I ate three-eighths of the pizza.

   I ate two-eighths of the pizza.

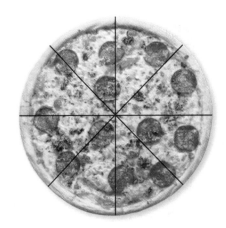

Simplifying Fractions

Name _____

Key Concept and Vocabulary

Factor and cancel to simplify.

1 $\dfrac{4}{6}$ Not simplified

2 $\dfrac{2 \times 2}{2 \times 3}$ Factor.

3 $\dfrac{\cancel{2} \times 2}{\cancel{2} \times 3}$ Cancel.

4 $\dfrac{2}{3}$ Simplified

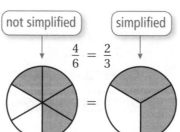

not simplified   simplified

$\dfrac{4}{6} = \dfrac{2}{3}$

Simplified fractions have smaller numbers.

PRACTICE MAKES *PURR*-FECT™

Check your answers at BigIdeasMath.com.

Simplify the fraction.

Fraction Model	Not Simplified	Factor and Cancel	Simplified
1.	$\dfrac{2}{6}$		
2.	$\dfrac{6}{8}$		
3.	$\dfrac{4}{10}$		
4.	$\dfrac{2}{8}$		
5.	$\dfrac{5}{10}$		

Estimating with Fractions

Name _____

Key Concept and Vocabulary

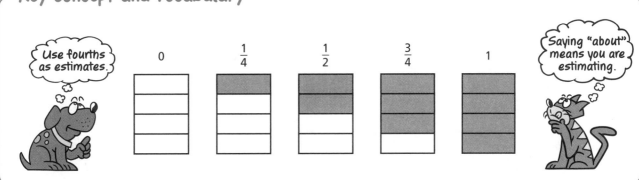

Use fourths as estimates.

Saying "about" means you are estimating.

0     $\frac{1}{4}$ $\frac{1}{2}$ $\frac{3}{4}$ 1

PRACTICE MAKES *PURR*-FECT™

Check your answers at BigIdeasMath.com.

Circle the best estimate for the shaded part.

1.

0     $\frac{1}{4}$ $\frac{1}{2}$ $\frac{3}{4}$ 1

2.

0     $\frac{1}{4}$ $\frac{1}{2}$ $\frac{3}{4}$ 1

3.

0     $\frac{1}{4}$ $\frac{1}{2}$ $\frac{3}{4}$ 1

4.

0     $\frac{1}{4}$ $\frac{1}{2}$ $\frac{3}{4}$ 1

5.

0     $\frac{1}{4}$ $\frac{1}{2}$ $\frac{3}{4}$ 1

6.

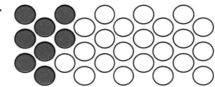

0     $\frac{1}{4}$ $\frac{1}{2}$ $\frac{3}{4}$ 1

7. GEESE IN FORMATION Estimate the fraction of the geese that are blue.

about [ ]

Comparing Fractions

Name _____

A number line helps compare fractions.

$\frac{1}{4}$ is less than $\frac{3}{8}$.

$\frac{1}{4} < \frac{3}{8}$

$\frac{3}{8}$ is greater than $\frac{1}{4}$.

$\frac{3}{8} > \frac{1}{4}$

$\frac{1}{4}$ is to the left of $\frac{3}{8}$. So, it is less.

$$0 \quad \frac{1}{8} \quad \frac{1}{4} \quad \frac{3}{8} \quad \frac{1}{2} \quad \frac{5}{8} \quad \frac{3}{4} \quad \frac{7}{8} \quad 1$$

PRACTICE MAKES PURR-FECT™

Check your answers at BigIdeasMath.com.

Draw a ● for each fraction. Then write "<" or ">" in ▢.

1. $\frac{1}{8}$ ▢ $\frac{5}{8}$

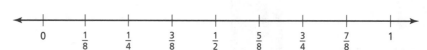

2. $\frac{3}{4}$ ▢ $\frac{5}{8}$

3. $\frac{7}{8}$ ▢ $\frac{3}{4}$

4. $\frac{1}{4}$ ▢ $\frac{1}{8}$

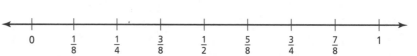

5. **RULER** Write the correct fractions on the ruler.

6. **WINDSHIELD** The blue car's windshield is three-eighths inch thick. The green car's windshield is one-half inch thick. Which is thicker? Circle your answer.

Blue   Green

Adding Like Fractions

Name _____

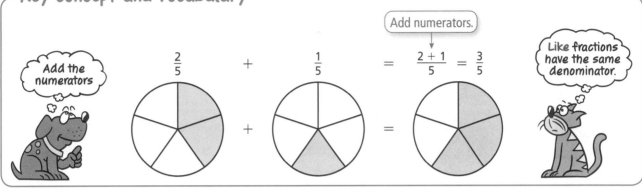

PRACTICE MAKES *PURR*-FECT™

Check your answers at BigIdeasMath.com.

Shade the sum. Then add the fractions. Show your work in ▢.

1.

$$\frac{\square}{\square} + \frac{\square}{\square} = \frac{\square + \square}{\square} = \frac{\square}{\square}$$

2.

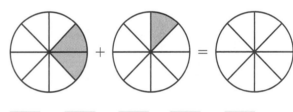

$$\frac{\square}{\square} + \frac{\square}{\square} = \frac{\square + \square}{\square} = \frac{\square}{\square}$$

3.

$$\frac{\square}{\square} + \frac{\square}{\square} = \frac{\square + \square}{\square} = \frac{\square}{\square}$$

4.

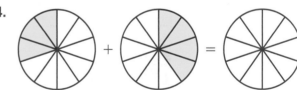

$$\frac{\square}{\square} + \frac{\square}{\square} = \frac{\square + \square}{\square} = \frac{\square}{\square}$$

5. BOOK THICKNESS Each cover of a book is one-eighth inch thick. The pages are five-eighths inch thick. How thick is the book?

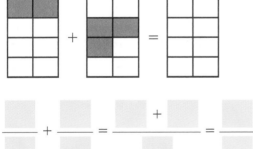

$$\frac{\square}{\square} + \frac{\square}{\square} + \frac{\square}{\square} = \frac{\square}{\square} \text{ in.}$$

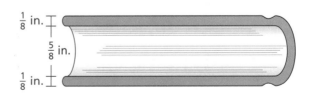

$\frac{1}{8}$ in.

$\frac{5}{8}$ in.

$\frac{1}{8}$ in.

Subtracting Like Fractions

Name _____

Key Concept and Vocabulary

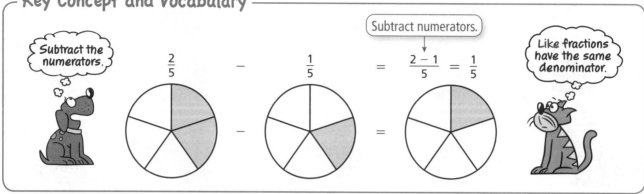

PRACTICE MAKES *PURR*-FECT™

Check your answers at BigIdeasMath.com.

Shade the difference. Then subtract the fractions. Show your work in ☐ **.**

1.

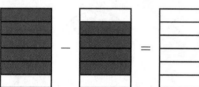

$$\frac{}{} - \frac{}{} = \frac{}{} = \frac{}{}$$

2.

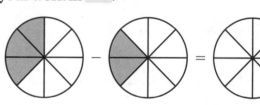

$$\frac{}{} - \frac{}{} = \frac{}{} = \frac{}{}$$

3.

$$\frac{}{} - \frac{}{} = \frac{}{} = \frac{}{}$$

4.

$$\frac{}{} - \frac{}{} = \frac{}{} = \frac{}{}$$

5. MOWING THE LAWN You have mowed about three-fourths of the lawn. How much do you have left?

$$\frac{4}{4} - \frac{}{} = \frac{}{}$$

↑

$\frac{4}{4}$ is one whole.

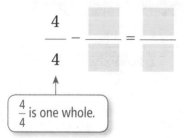

Key Concept and Vocabulary

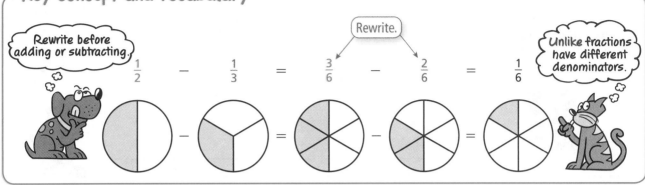

Rewrite before adding or subtracting.

Rewrite.

Unlike fractions have different denominators.

$$\frac{1}{2} - \frac{1}{3} = \frac{3}{6} - \frac{2}{6} = \frac{1}{6}$$

PRACTICE MAKES *PURR*-FECT™

Check your answers at BigIdeasMath.com.

Shade the sum or difference. Then add or subtract the fractions. Show your work in ▢.

1.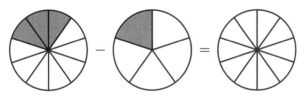

____ + ____ = ____ + ____ = ____

2.

____ + ____ = ____ + ____ = ____

3.

____ − ____ = ____ − ____ = ____

4.

____ − ____ = ____ − ____ = ____

5. **QUESADILLA** You eat one-fourth of the quesadilla. Later, you eat one-third of what is left. How much of the quesadilla do you eat? Circle the correct answer.

less than half

exactly half

more than half

Multiplying Fractions

Name _____

Key Concept and Vocabulary

Multiply numerators and denominators.

Cancel common factors.

$$\frac{1}{3} \times \frac{3}{4} = \frac{1 \times \cancel{3}}{\cancel{3} \times 4} = \frac{1}{4}$$

$\frac{1}{3}$ of

=

$\frac{1}{3}$ of $\frac{3}{4}$ means $\frac{1}{3}$ times $\frac{3}{4}$.

PRACTICE MAKES *PURR*-FECT™

Check your answers at BigIdeasMath.com.

Shade the product. Write the problem in ____.

1.

$\frac{1}{2}$ of

=

_____ × _____ = _____

2.

$\frac{2}{3}$ of

=

_____ × _____ = _____

3.

$\frac{3}{5}$ of

=

_____ × _____ = _____

4.

$\frac{1}{3}$ of

=

_____ × _____ = _____

5. RECIPE A recipe for muffins needs three-fourths of a cup of milk. You are making half of the recipe. How much milk should you use?

_____ cup

1 cup —

½ —

—

Improper Fractions

Name _____

PRACTICE MAKES *PURR*-FECT™

Check your answers at BigIdeasMath.com.

1. Circle the fractions that are *improper*.

$\frac{1}{3}$ $\frac{5}{3}$ $\frac{5}{2}$ $\frac{10}{11}$ $\frac{6}{12}$ $\frac{7}{7}$

2. Circle the correct words.

∴ The numerator is *less than* the denominator.　　proper fraction　　improper fraction

∴ The numerator is *equal to* the denominator.　　proper fraction　　improper fraction

∴ The numerator is *greater than* the denominator.　　proper fraction　　improper fraction

Graph ● the fraction on the number line.

3. $\frac{7}{4}$

0　$\frac{1}{4}$　$\frac{1}{2}$　$\frac{3}{4}$　1　$\frac{5}{4}$　$\frac{3}{2}$　$\frac{7}{4}$　2

4. $\frac{9}{8}$

0　$\frac{1}{4}$　$\frac{1}{2}$　$\frac{3}{4}$　1　$\frac{5}{4}$　$\frac{3}{2}$　$\frac{7}{4}$　2

5. **PICKUPS** Which pickup can carry more sand? Circle the correct answer.

Three-quarter ton

Three-halves ton

One ton

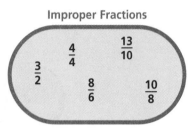

One ton

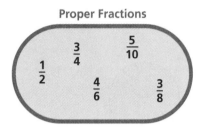

Three-halves ton

Three-quarter ton

Mixed Numbers

Name _____

Key Concept and Vocabulary

Mixed numbers have two parts.

Improper fraction	Sum	Mixed number

$$\frac{5}{3} = \frac{3}{3} + \frac{2}{3} = 1\frac{2}{3}$$

A mixed number is a sum: (whole) + (part).

PRACTICE MAKES *PURR*-FECT™

Check your answers at BigIdeasMath.com.

Write the improper fraction as a mixed number.

	Improper fraction	Sum	Mixed number

1.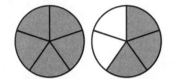

$$\frac{8}{5} = \frac{\ }{\ } + \frac{\ }{\ } = \square\frac{\ }{\ }$$

2.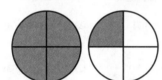

$$\frac{5}{4} = \frac{\ }{\ } + \frac{\ }{\ } = \square\frac{\ }{\ }$$

3.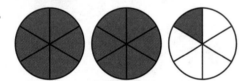

$$\frac{13}{6} = \frac{\ }{\ } + \frac{\ }{\ } = \square\frac{\ }{\ }$$

4.

$$\frac{7}{2} = \frac{\ }{\ } + \frac{\ }{\ } = \square\frac{\ }{\ }$$

5. **MEASURING CUPS** A cinnamon roll recipe needs 7 cups of flour. You are making a half recipe. Circle *all* statements that are true.

You need $\frac{7}{2}$ cups flour.

You need $\frac{2}{7}$ cup flour.

You need $3\frac{1}{2}$ cups flour.

$\frac{1}{3}$ cup $\frac{1}{2}$ cup

$\frac{1}{4}$ cup   1 cup

$\frac{1}{8}$ cup

Key Concept and Vocabulary

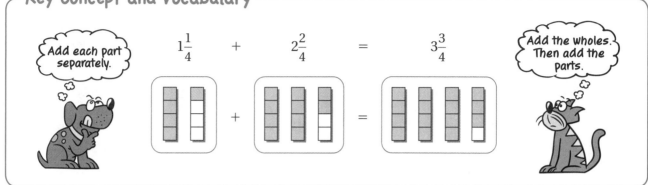

Add each part separately.

$$1\frac{1}{4} \quad + \quad 2\frac{2}{4} \quad = \quad 3\frac{3}{4}$$

Add the wholes. Then add the parts.

PRACTICE MAKES *PURR-FECT*™

Check your answers at BigIdeasMath.com.

Add the mixed numbers. Write the problem in ▢ **.**

1.

$$\frac{}{} + \frac{}{} = \frac{}{}$$

2.

$$\frac{}{} + \frac{}{} = \frac{}{}$$

3.

$$\frac{}{} + \frac{}{} = \frac{}{}$$

4.

$$\frac{}{} + \frac{}{} = \frac{}{}$$

5. **FOOTBALL** The football team needs 10 yards to make a first down. Does the team make a first down?

$$1\frac{1}{4} \text{ yd} + 2\frac{1}{4} \text{ yd} + 3\frac{1}{4} \text{ yd} + 3\frac{1}{4} \text{ yd} = \boxed{} \text{ yd}$$

Yes, it makes a first down.

No, it does not make a first down.

Subtracting Mixed Numbers

Name _____

Key Concept and Vocabulary

 Subtract each part separately.

$$3\frac{3}{4} \quad - \quad 1\frac{1}{4} \quad = \quad 2\frac{2}{4}$$

Subtract the wholes. Then subtract the parts.

PRACTICE MAKES *PURR*-FECT™

Check your answers at BigIdeasMath.com.

Subtract the mixed numbers. Write the problem in .

1.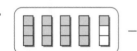

$$\dfrac{\quad}{\quad} - \dfrac{\quad}{\quad} = \dfrac{\quad}{\quad}$$

2.

$$\dfrac{\quad}{\quad} - \dfrac{\quad}{\quad} = \dfrac{\quad}{\quad}$$

3.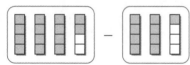

$$\dfrac{\quad}{\quad} - \dfrac{\quad}{\quad} = \dfrac{\quad}{\quad}$$

4.

$$\dfrac{\quad}{\quad} - \dfrac{\quad}{\quad} = \dfrac{\quad}{\quad}$$

5. **PICTURE** With the frame, the picture is 10 inches wide. How wide is the picture *without* the frame?

in.

6. **PICTURE** Estimate the length of the picture with the frame.

in.

$1\frac{1}{4}$ in.

10 in.

$1\frac{1}{4}$ in.

Decimal Place Value

Name _____

Key Concept and Vocabulary

Look for the decimal point.

thousands
hundreds
tens
ones

6,281.

Six thousand two hundred eighty-one

thousandths
hundredths
tenths

0.341

Three hundred forty-one thousandths

Decimals remind me of money.

PRACTICE MAKES *PURR*-FECT™

Check your answers at BigIdeasMath.com.

Write the value of the check in words.

1.

Jane Doe
123 Anytown Ave
Anytown, USA   1001

DATE _____

PAY
TO THE
ORDER OF ___Electric Company___ $ |271.53|

_____ DOLLARS

Your Financial Institution
Address of Your Financial Institution
City, State   12345

FOR _____   *Jane Doe*

⑆123456789⑆ ⑈1234567⑈ 1001

2.

Jane Doe
123 Anytown Ave
Anytown, USA   1002

DATE _____

PAY
TO THE
ORDER OF ___Mortgage Company___ $ |1050.90|

_____ DOLLARS

Your Financial Institution
Address of Your Financial Institution
City, State   12345

FOR _____   *Jane Doe*

⑆123456789⑆ ⑈1234567⑈ 1002

Write the price of gas in words.

3.

UNLEADED

GAS 3.49⁹

4.

UNLEADED

GAS 2.58⁹

Write the words as a decimal.

5. Three and four tenths

6. Fifteen and thirty-seven hundredths

7. How many miles has the car driven?
(Write your answer in words.)

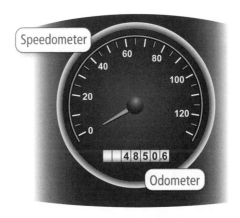

Speedometer

40 60 80
20   100
0   120

| 4 8 5 0 6 |

Odometer

Comparing Decimals

Name _____

Key Concept and Vocabulary

A number line helps compare decimals.

0.4 is less than 0.5.

0.4 < 0.5

0.5 is greater than 0.4.

0.5 > 0.4

0.4 is to the left of 0.5. So, it is less.

0   0.1   0.2   0.3   0.4   0.5   0.6   0.7   0.8   0.9   1

PRACTICE MAKES PURR-FECT™

Check your answers at BigIdeasMath.com.

Draw a ● **for each decimal. Then write "<" or ">" in** ▢.

1. 0.3 ▢ 0.2

0   0.1   0.2   0.3   0.4   0.5   0.6   0.7   0.8   0.9   1

2. 1.7 ▢ 1.8

1   1.1   1.2   1.3   1.4   1.5   1.6   1.7   1.8   1.9   2

3. 2.35 ▢ 2.4

2   2.1   2.2   2.3   2.4   2.5   2.6   2.7   2.8   2.9   3

4. 3.7 ▢ 3.55

3   3.1   3.2   3.3   3.4   3.5   3.6   3.7   3.8   3.9   4

5. Write the decimals that are shown on the number line.

4   4.1   4.2   4.3   4.4   4.5   4.6   4.7   4.8   4.9   5

● = ▢

● = ▢

● = ▢

6. APPLES AND ORANGES Which weighs more, the apples or the oranges? Circle the correct answer.

Apples weigh more.

Oranges weigh more.

Fractions and Decimals

Name _____

PRACTICE MAKES *PURR*-FECT™

Check your answers at BigIdeasMath.com.

Draw a line from the decimal to its fraction.

1. 0.6　　　　**2.** 0.25　　　　**3.** 0.5　　　　**4.** 0.75

$\frac{1}{4} =$ 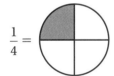　　　$\frac{3}{4} =$ 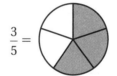　　　$\frac{3}{5} =$ 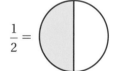　　　$\frac{1}{2} =$

5. NUMBER LINE Write 0.375 as a simplified fraction.

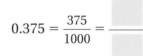

0　0.1　0.2　0.3　0.4　0.5　0.6　0.7　0.8　0.9　1

$0.375 = \dfrac{375}{1000} = \dfrac{}{}$

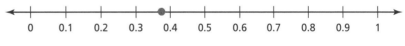

0　$\frac{1}{8}$　$\frac{1}{4}$　$\frac{3}{8}$　$\frac{1}{2}$　$\frac{5}{8}$　$\frac{3}{4}$　$\frac{7}{8}$　1

6. CARPENTRY Carpenters use a fraction-decimal chart to help change fractions to decimals. Use the chart to write the fraction $\frac{3}{16}$ as a decimal.

$\frac{3}{16} = $

Common Fraction-Decimal Conversion			
$\frac{1}{16} = 0.0625$	$\frac{5}{16} = 0.3125$	$\frac{9}{16} = 0.5625$	$\frac{13}{16} = 0.8125$
$\frac{1}{8} = 0.125$	$\frac{3}{8} = 0.375$	$\frac{5}{8} = 0.625$	$\frac{7}{8} = 0.875$
$\frac{3}{16} = 0.1875$	$\frac{7}{16} = 0.4375$	$\frac{11}{16} = 0.6875$	$\frac{15}{16} = 0.9375$
$\frac{1}{4} = 0.25$	$\frac{1}{2} = 0.5$	$\frac{3}{4} = 0.75$	

　　　Basic Skills Topic 8.3　121

Rounding Decimals

Name _____

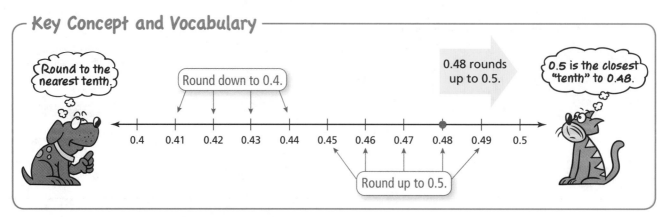

Round to the nearest tenth.

Round down to 0.4.

0.48 rounds up to 0.5.

0.5 is the closest "tenth" to 0.48.

0.4 0.41 0.42 0.43 0.44 0.45 0.46 0.47 0.48 0.49 0.5

Round up to 0.5.

PRACTICE MAKES *PURR*-FECT™

Check your answers at BigIdeasMath.com.

Circle the closest "tenth." Then write the answer in ▭.

1.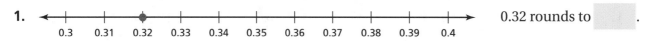

0.3 0.31 0.32 0.33 0.34 0.35 0.36 0.37 0.38 0.39 0.4

0.32 rounds to ▭.

2.

0.6 0.61 0.62 0.63 0.64 0.65 0.66 0.67 0.68 0.69 0.7

0.69 rounds to ▭.

3.

0.1 0.11 0.12 0.13 0.14 0.15 0.16 0.17 0.18 0.19 0.2

0.17 rounds to ▭.

4.

0.9 0.91 0.92 0.93 0.94 0.95 0.96 0.97 0.98 0.99 1.0

0.91 rounds to ▭.

Count the money. Circle the better statement.

5.

The total is about $0.40.

The total is about $0.30.

6.

The total is about $0.40.

The total is about $0.30.

7. COINS Draw lines to match the coin to the closest price.

$0.08 $0.49 $0.02 $0.04 $0.27

Estimating with Decimals

Name _____

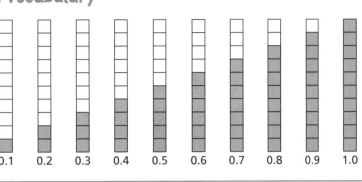

PRACTICE MAKES *PURR*-FECT™

Check your answers at BigIdeasMath.com.

To the nearest tenth, estimate how much of the figure is shaded. Write ▢ as a decimal.

1.

Shaded Part

2.

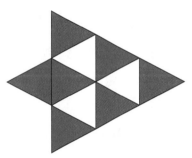

Shaded Part

3.

Shaded Part

4.

Shaded Part

5. **HIDDEN WORD PUZZLE** Shade the letters that form a hidden word. What is the word?

6. **HIDDEN WORD PUZZLE** Estimate how much of the puzzle is shaded.

Shaded Part

Name _____

Key Concept and Vocabulary

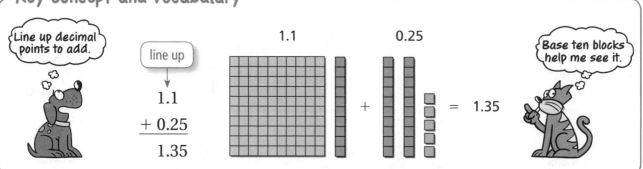

Line up decimal points to add.

line up

$$\begin{array}{r} 1.1 \\ + \ 0.25 \\ \hline 1.35 \end{array}$$

1.1   0.25

+ = 1.35

Base ten blocks help me see it.

PRACTICE MAKES *PURR*-FECT™

Check your answers at BigIdeasMath.com.

Write the decimal addition in ▭.

1. + =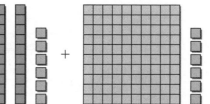

2.  +  +  =

Add the two decimals. Show your work in ▭.

3. 3.45 and 2.06

4. 5.3 and 1.58

5. 6.02 and 5.48

6. 11.4 and 8.6

7. **MONEY** How much money do you have in your left and right pockets?

   $ _____

   + $ _____

   ─────────

   $ _____

Left Pocket

+

Right Pocket

Subtracting Decimals

Name _____

Key Concept and Vocabulary

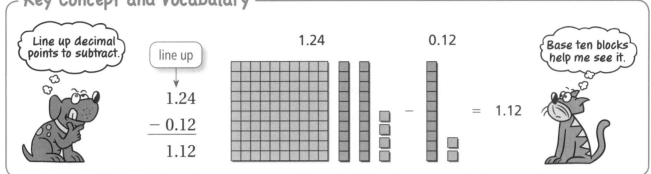

Line up decimal points to subtract.

line up

$$\begin{array}{r} 1.24 \\ -\ 0.12 \\ \hline 1.12 \end{array}$$

1.24   0.12

− = 1.12

Base ten blocks help me see it.

PRACTICE MAKES *PURR*-FECT™

Check your answers at BigIdeasMath.com.

Write the decimal subtraction in ▢.

1.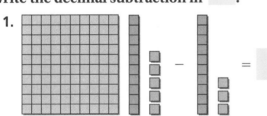

− =

2.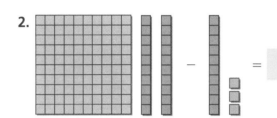

− =

Subtract the decimals. Show your work in ▢.

3. $3.45 - 2.05$

4. $5.3 - 1.6$

5. $6.52 - 5.42$

6. $11.6 - 8.6$

7. SHOPPING You bought a baseball cap, sunglasses, and some lip balm. How much of $20 do you have left?

$ _____
$ _____
+ $ _____
─────────
$ _____

$ 20.00
− $ _____
─────────
$ _____

$5.95

$7.95

$2.95

Multiplying Decimals

Name _____

Key Concept and Vocabulary

"Add the number of decimal points."

$$1.2 \longleftarrow \text{1 decimal place}$$
$$\underline{\times\, 0.5} \longleftarrow +\text{1 decimal place}$$
$$0.6\,0 \longleftarrow \text{2 decimal places}$$

$0.5 \times$ ▮ = ▮

"0.5 times" is the same as "one half of."

PRACTICE MAKES *PURR*-FECT™

Check your answers at BigIdeasMath.com.

Write the decimal in ▮ **.**

1. ▢ × ▮ = ▮

2. ▢ × ▮ = ▮

Multiply the decimals.

3. (one-half of)
    $$1.4$$
    $$\underline{\times\, 0.5}$$

4. (one-tenth of)
    $$350$$
    $$\underline{\times\, 0.1}$$

5. (one-quarter of)
    $$2.4$$
    $$\underline{\times\, 0.2\,5}$$

6. (one-fifth of)
    $$5\,0$$
    $$\underline{\times\, 0.2}$$

7. **CENTIMETERS** To change inches to centimeters, multiply by 2.54. Change three-quarters of an inch to centimeters.

    2.54 ← (conversion factor)
    $$\underline{\times\, 0.75}$$ ← (three-quarters inch)

    _____
    centimeters

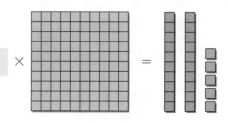

0.75 in.

Percents

Key Concept and Vocabulary

Percent means "per hundred."

$$30\% = \frac{30}{100}$$

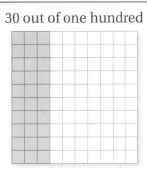

30
per
cent

30 out of one hundred

A century is 100 years.

PRACTICE MAKES *PURR*-FECT™

Check your answers at BigIdeasMath.com.

Write the percent in [ ] **.**

1.

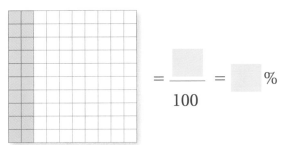

$$= \frac{\boxed{}}{100} = \boxed{}\%$$

2.

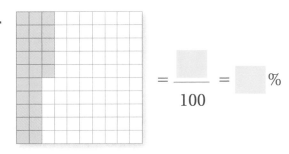

$$= \frac{\boxed{}}{100} = \boxed{}\%$$

3.

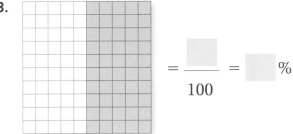

$$= \frac{\boxed{}}{100} = \boxed{}\%$$

4.

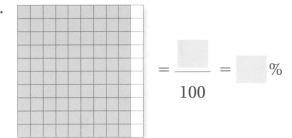

$$= \frac{\boxed{}}{100} = \boxed{}\%$$

5. **SONGBIRDS** One hundred people were asked to name their favorite songbird. Estimate the percent for each category.

Robin = [ ] %

Dove = [ ] %

Cardinal = [ ] %

Other = [ ] %

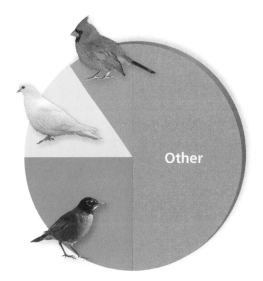

Other

Percents and Fractions

Name _____

Key Concept and Vocabulary

Percent means "per hundred."

$$25\% = \frac{25}{100}$$

$$= \frac{25 \times 1}{25 \times 4}$$

$$= \frac{1}{4}$$

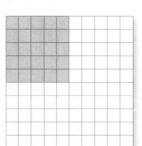

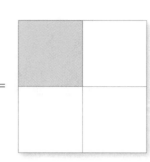

To simplify a fraction, factor and cancel.

PRACTICE MAKES PURR-FECT™

Check your answers at BigIdeasMath.com.

Write the percent as a simplified fraction.

1.

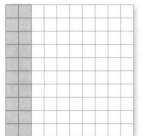

$$= \frac{\boxed{}}{100} = \frac{\boxed{}}{\boxed{}}$$

2.

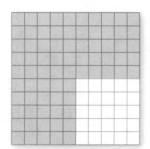

$$= \frac{\boxed{}}{100} = \frac{\boxed{}}{\boxed{}}$$

3.

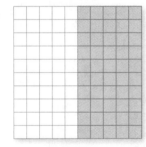

$$= \frac{\boxed{}}{100} = \frac{\boxed{}}{\boxed{}}$$

4.

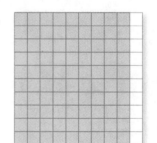

$$= \frac{\boxed{}}{100} = \frac{\boxed{}}{\boxed{}}$$

5. **DOG TRICKS** Owners of twenty dogs were surveyed. Eight of the dogs knew the trick "roll over." Write this fraction as a percent.

$$\frac{\boxed{}}{20} = \frac{5 \times \boxed{}}{5 \times 20}$$

$$= \frac{\boxed{}}{100}$$

$$= \boxed{}\%$$

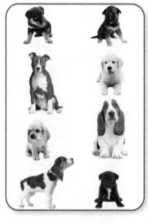

Can roll over

Cannot roll over

Percents and Decimals

Name _____

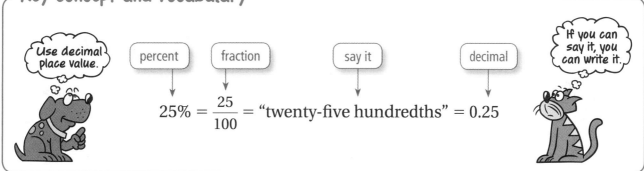
PRACTICE MAKES *PURR*-FECT™

Check your answers at BigIdeasMath.com.

Write the percent as a decimal.

1.

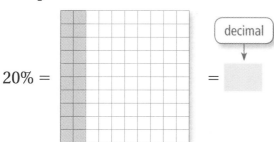

$20\% =$ decimal $=$ [ ]

2.

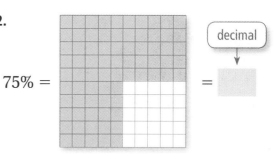

$75\% =$ decimal $=$ [ ]

Write the decimal as a percent.

3.

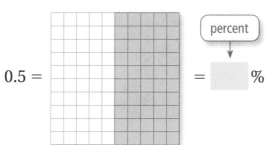

$0.5 =$ percent $=$ [ ] %

4.

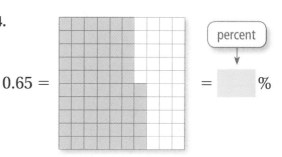

$0.65 =$ percent $=$ [ ] %

5. 737 An empty 737 jet weighs about 60,000 pounds. About 35% of this weight is in the wings. Write this percent as a decimal.

$35\% =$ [ ]

6. 737 Estimate how much the wings weigh.

[ ] lb

737 Jet
60,000 lb

Percent of a Number

Name _____

Key Concept and Vocabulary

Multiply to find a percent.

Percent → Write as decimal. → Multiply.

$25\% \text{ of } 8 = 0.25 \times 8 = 2$

25% of 8

25% is the same as one-fourth.

PRACTICE MAKES *PURR*-FECT™

Check your answers at BigIdeasMath.com.

Write the 6% sales tax for the item.

1.

$\begin{array}{r} 30 \\ \times \\ \hline \end{array}$

$ ____ Sales Tax

2.

$\begin{array}{r} 20 \\ \times \\ \hline \end{array}$

$ ____ Sales Tax

3.

$\begin{array}{r} 15 \\ \times \\ \hline \end{array}$

$ ____ Sales Tax

4.

$\begin{array}{r} 50 \\ \times \\ \hline \end{array}$

$ ____ Sales Tax

5. SWIMMING Only 30% of Americans swim well enough to swim 100 yards. Of 200 Americans, how many would you say can swim 100 yards?

$\begin{array}{r} 200 \\ \times \\ \hline \end{array}$

Angles

Name _____

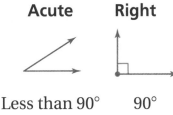

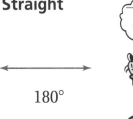
PRACTICE MAKES *PURR*-FECT™

Check your answers at BigIdeasMath.com.

Write the degree measure of the angle. Is it *acute*, *right*, *obtuse*, or *straight*? Circle the answer.

1. ____°

Acute

Right

Obtuse

Straight

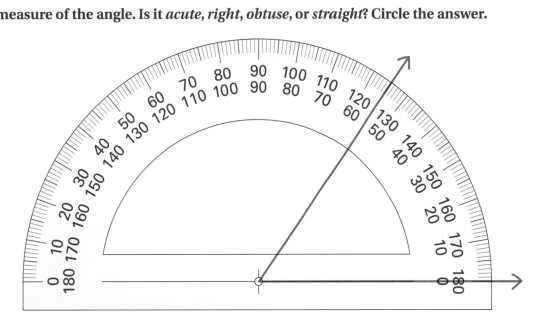

2. ____°

Acute

Right

Obtuse

Straight

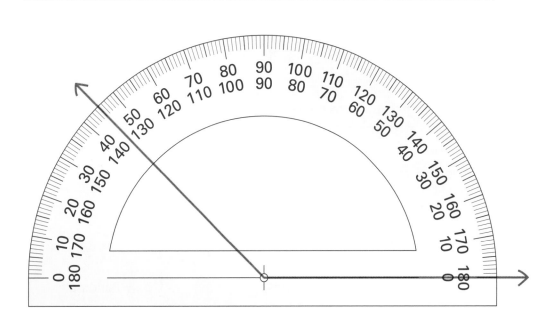

Rectangles and Triangles

Name _____

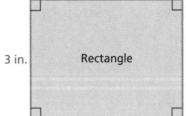
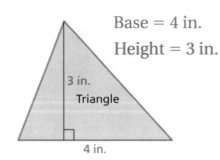

PRACTICE MAKES *PURR*-FECT™

Check your answers at BigIdeasMath.com.

Write the base and height of the figure.

1.

6 in.

8 in.

Base = ⬜ in.   Height = ⬜ in.

2.

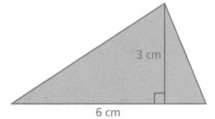

3 cm

6 cm

Base = ⬜ cm   Height = ⬜ cm

3.

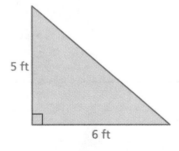

5 ft

6 ft

Base = ⬜ ft   Height = ⬜ ft

4.

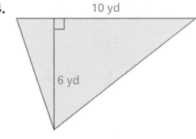

10 yd

6 yd

Base = ⬜ yd   Height = ⬜ yd

How many of the prism's faces are rectangles? How many faces are triangles?

5.

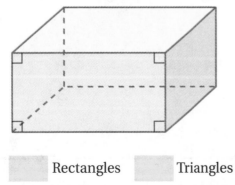

⬜ Rectangles   ⬜ Triangles

6.

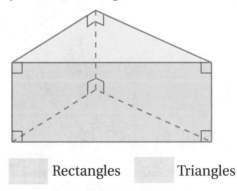

⬜ Rectangles   ⬜ Triangles

Parallelograms and Trapezoids

Name _____

Key Concept and Vocabulary

Parallelograms have 4 sides.

Parallelogram

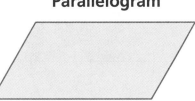

2 sets of parallel sides

Trapezoid

1 set of parallel sides

Trapezoids have 4 sides.

PRACTICE MAKES *PURR*-FECT™

Check your answers at BigIdeasMath.com.

Is the figure a *parallelogram*, a *trapezoid*, or *neither*? Circle the correct answer.

1.

Parallelogram   Trapezoid   Neither

2.

Parallelogram   Trapezoid   Neither

3.

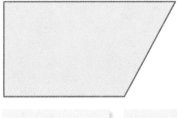

Parallelogram   Trapezoid   Neither

4.

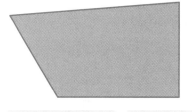

Parallelogram   Trapezoid   Neither

5. **PARALLELOGRAM LIFT** Why is this called a parallelogram lift?

6. **PARALLELOGRAM LIFT** Trace the parallelogram in the lift.

Circles

Name _____

The radius is half the width.

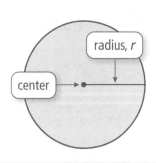

center → • radius, *r*

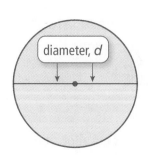

diameter, *d*

The diameter is twice the radius.

PRACTICE MAKES PURR-FECT™

Check your answers at BigIdeasMath.com.

Write the radius and the diameter.

1.

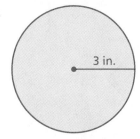

3 in.

Radius = _____ in.   Diameter = _____ in.

2.

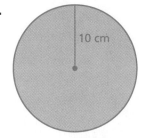

10 cm

Radius = _____ cm   Diameter = _____ cm

3.

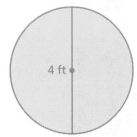

4 ft

Radius = _____ ft   Diameter = _____ ft

4.

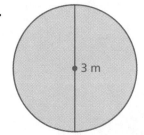

3 m

Radius = _____ m   Diameter = _____ m

5. BASKETBALL COURT Write the radius and diameter of the center circle on a basketball court.

Radius = _____ ft

Diameter = _____ ft

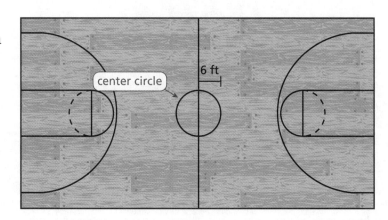

center circle

6 ft

Perimeter

Name _____

Key Concept and Vocabulary

Add the side lengths.

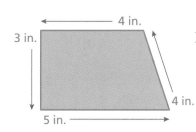

Perimeter = 3 + 5 + 4 + 4

= 16 in.

Perimeter is the distance around.

PRACTICE MAKES *PURR*-FECT™

Check your answers at BigIdeasMath.com.

Write the perimeter of the figure in ▢. Include the units in your answer.

1.

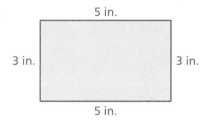

5 in.

3 in.   3 in.

5 in.

Perimeter = ▢

2.

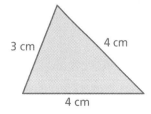

3 cm   4 cm

4 cm

Perimeter = ▢

3.

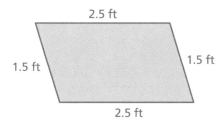

2.5 ft

1.5 ft   1.5 ft

2.5 ft

Perimeter = ▢

4.

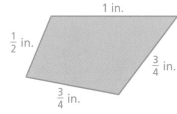

1 in.

$\frac{1}{2}$ in.

$\frac{3}{4}$ in.

$\frac{3}{4}$ in.

Perimeter = ▢

5. PASTURE FENCE Find the perimeter of the pasture.

Perimeter = ▢

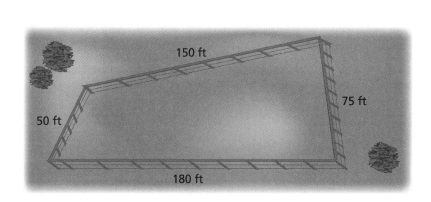

150 ft

75 ft

50 ft

180 ft

6. PASTURE FENCE You have 450 feet of fencing. Do you have enough to fence the pasture?

Yes   No

Area

Name _____

Key Concept and Vocabulary

Rectangle:
Area = bh

Area = Base × Height
= 4 × 3
= 12 in.²

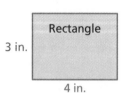

Rectangle

3 in.

4 in.

Area = $\frac{1}{2}$ (Base × Height)

= $\frac{1}{2}$(4 × 3)

= 6 in.²

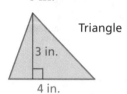

Triangle

3 in.

4 in.

Triangle:
Area = $\frac{1}{2}$ bh

PRACTICE MAKES *PURR*-FECT™

Check your answers at BigIdeasMath.com.

Write the area of the figure in [ ]. Include the units in your answer.

1.

6 in.

8 in.

Area =

2.

3 cm

6 cm

Area =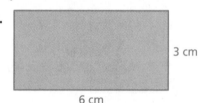

3.

6 in.

8 in.

Area =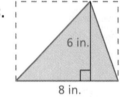

4.

3 cm

6 cm

Area =

5. WATERCOLOR Find the area of the iguana painting.

Area =

6. WATERCOLOR If you doubled the base and the height, what is the area?

Area =

2 ft

3 ft

Circumference of a Circle

Name _____

Key Concept and Vocabulary

C is the distance around a circle.

Pi

$\pi \approx 3.14$

$C = \pi d$

$\approx 3.14 \times 2$

$= 6.28$ in.

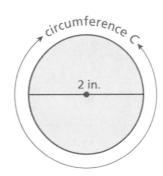

circumference C

2 in.

π is about 3.14.

PRACTICE MAKES PURR-FECT™

Check your answers at BigIdeasMath.com.

Find the circumference of the circle. Include the units in your anwer.

1.

4 ft

$C = \pi d$

$\approx 3.14 \times$ ▢

$=$ ▢

2.

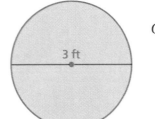

3 ft

$C = \pi d$

$\approx 3.14 \times$ ▢

$=$ ▢

3.

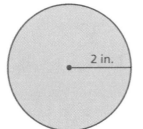

2 in.

$C = \pi d$

$\approx 3.14 \times$ ▢

$=$ ▢

4.

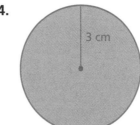

3 cm

$C = \pi d$

$\approx 3.14 \times$ ▢

$=$ ▢

5. CIRCULAR SAW Find the circumference of the circular saw blade.

Circumference $\approx$ ▢

6. CIRCULAR SAW The blade has two teeth per inch. How many teeth are on the blade?

Number of teeth $\approx$ ▢

18.0v

7 in.

Area of a Circle

Name _____

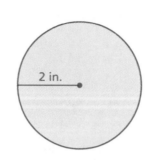

PRACTICE MAKES *PURR*-FECT™

Check your answers at BigIdeasMath.com.

Find the area of the circle. Include the units in your answer.

1.

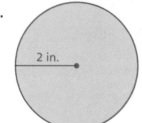

2 in.

$A = \pi r^2$

$\approx 3.14 \times$ ___

$=$ ___

2.

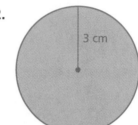

3 cm

$A = \pi r^2$

$\approx 3.14 \times$ ___

$=$ ___

3.

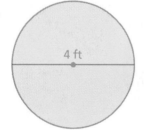

4 ft

$A = \pi r^2$

$\approx 3.14 \times$ ___

$=$ ___

4.

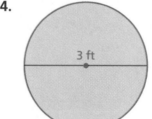

3 ft

$A = \pi r^2$

$\approx 3.14 \times$ ___

$=$ ___

5. STAINED GLASS Find the area of the stained glass window.

Area ≈ ___

6. COST The colored glass costs $0.25 per square inch. How much does it cost to buy the glass to make the stained glass window?

Cost ≈ $ ___

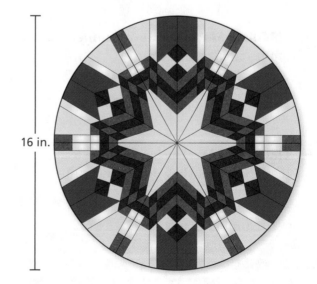

16 in.

Related Areas

Key Concept and Vocabulary

The areas of some polygons are related.

Triangle: $A = \frac{1}{2}bh$

Square: $A = b^2$

Rectangle: $A = bh$

Parallelogram: $A = bh$

Rhombus: $A = \frac{1}{2}d_1d_2$

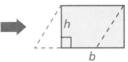

The area of a parallelogram is the area of a rectangle with the same base and height.

PRACTICE MAKES *PURR*-FECT™

Check your answers at BigIdeasMath.com.

1. **TRIANGLE** How does the area of each triangle compare to the area of the parallelogram?

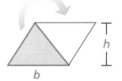

2. **SQUARE** How does the area of the square compare to the area of each triangle?

3. **RECTANGLE** How can you justify the area formula for a rectangle using a right triangle with the same base and height?

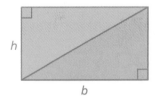

4. **RHOMBUS** How can you rearrange the four right triangles to justify the area formula for a rhombus?

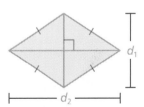

Three-Dimensional Figures

Name _____

Key Concept and Vocabulary

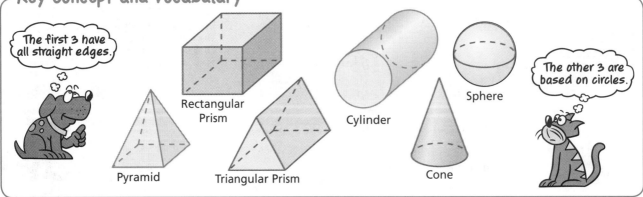

The first 3 have all straight edges.

Rectangular Prism

Pyramid

Triangular Prism

Cylinder

Cone

Sphere

The other 3 are based on circles.

PRACTICE MAKES *PURR*-FECT™

Check your answers at BigIdeasMath.com.

Name the basic shape of the building. *(Hint: There is one of each.)*

1.

2.

3.

4.

5.

6.

Faces, Edges, and Vertices

Name _____

Key Concept and Vocabulary

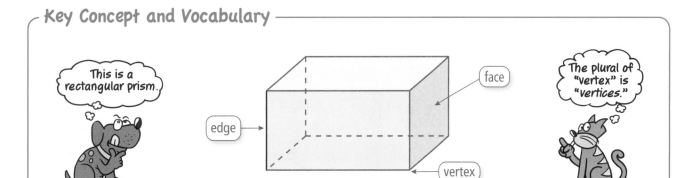

PRACTICE MAKES *PURR*-FECT™

Check your answers at BigIdeasMath.com.

Write the number of faces, edges, and vertices.

1.

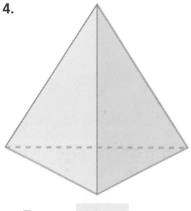

Faces = ⬚

Edges = ⬚

Vertices = ⬚

2.

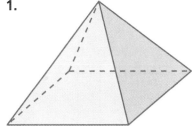

Faces = ⬚

Edges = ⬚

Vertices = ⬚

3.

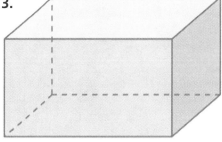

Faces = ⬚

Edges = ⬚

Vertices = ⬚

4.

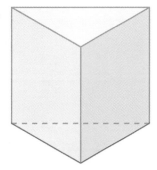

Faces = ⬚

Edges = ⬚

Vertices = ⬚

5.

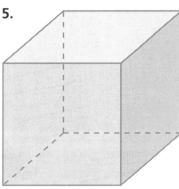

Faces = ⬚

Edges = ⬚

Vertices = ⬚

6.

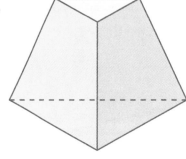

Faces = ⬚

Edges = ⬚

Vertices = ⬚

Surface Area of a Prism

Name _____

Key Concept and Vocabulary

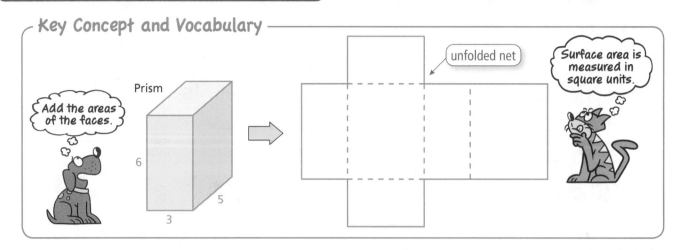

PRACTICE MAKES *PURR*-FECT™

Check your answers at BigIdeasMath.com.

Find the surface area of the prism. Include the units in your answer.

1.

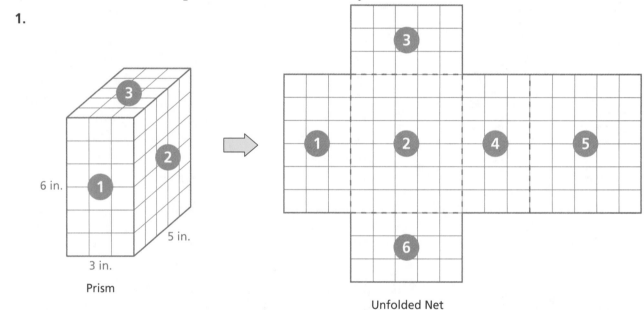

Prism

Unfolded Net

Key Concept and Vocabulary

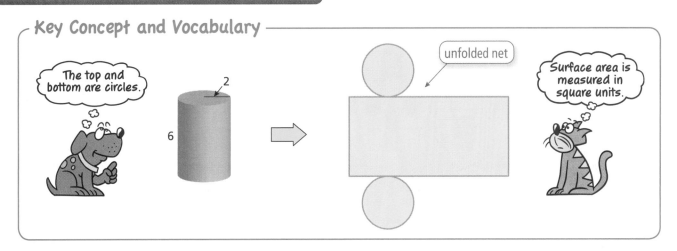

PRACTICE MAKES *PURR*-FECT™

Check your answers at BigIdeasMath.com.

Find the surface area of the cylinder. Include the units in your answer.

1.

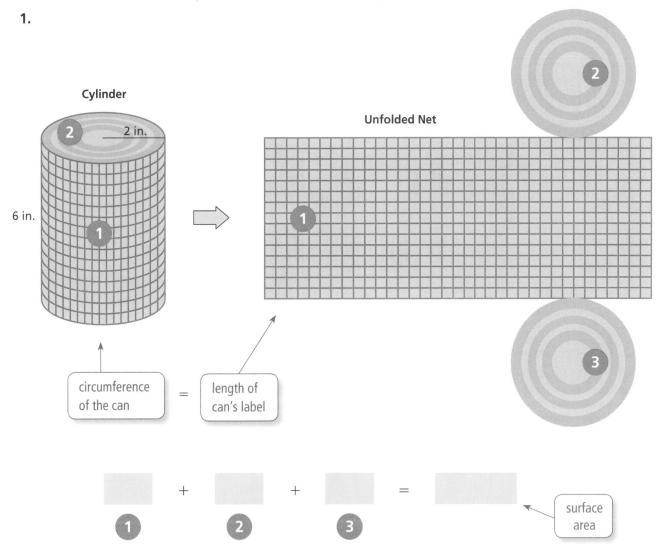

Volume by Counting

Name _____

Key Concept and Vocabulary

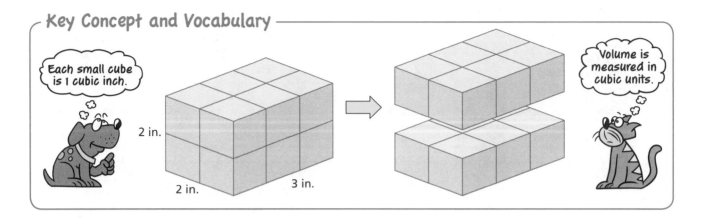

Each small cube is 1 cubic inch.

2 in.

2 in.   3 in.

Volume is measured in cubic units.

PRACTICE MAKES PURR-FECT™

Check your answers at BigIdeasMath.com.

Find the volume of the prism. Include the units in your answer.

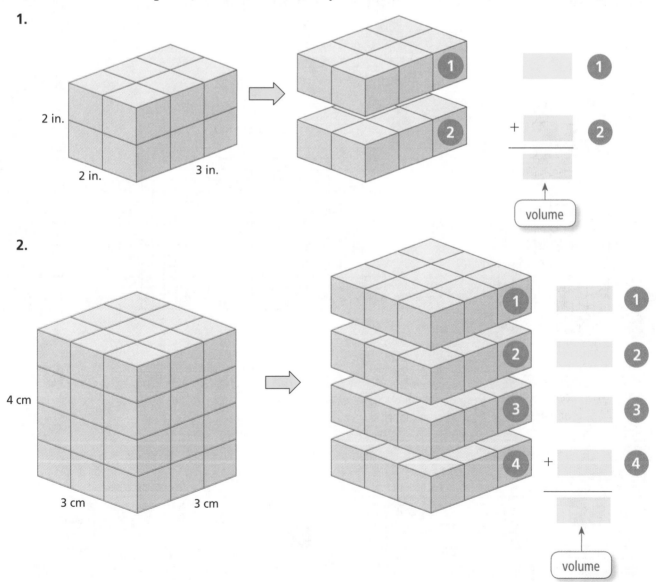

1.

2 in.

2 in.   3 in.

(1)

+   (2)

volume

2.

4 cm

3 cm   3 cm

(1)

(2)

(3)

+   (4)

volume

Volume of a Rectangular Prism

Name _____

Key Concept and Vocabulary

Volume is base area times height.

Base area = 3 × 2
= 6 in.²

base area   height

Volume = 6 × 2
= 12 in.³

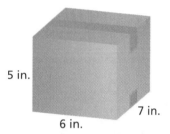

2 in.

2 in.

3 in.   base

Volume is measured in cubic units.

PRACTICE MAKES *PURR*-FECT™

Check your answers at BigIdeasMath.com.

Find the volume of the prism. Include the units in your answer.

1.

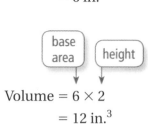

8 in.

6 in.

4 in.

Volume = ⬚ × ⬚ = ⬚

2.

5 in.

6 in.

7 in.

Volume = ⬚ × ⬚ = ⬚

3.

3 in.

8 in.   8 in.

Volume = ⬚ × ⬚ = ⬚

4.

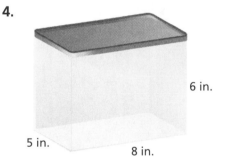

6 in.

5 in.

8 in.

Volume = ⬚ × ⬚ = ⬚

5. Circle the box that has the greatest volume.

Name _____

Key Concept and Vocabulary

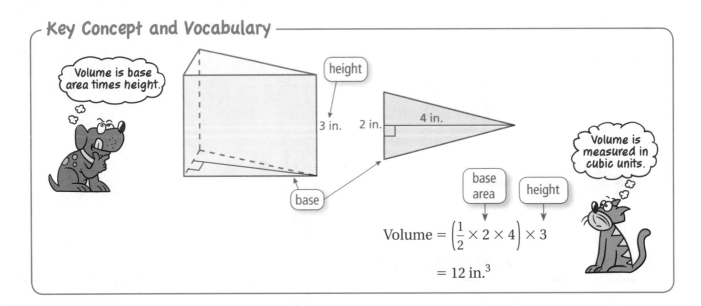

Volume is base area times height.

height

base

3 in. 2 in. 4 in.

Volume is measured in cubic units.

base area   height

$$\text{Volume} = \left(\frac{1}{2} \times 2 \times 4\right) \times 3$$

$$= 12 \text{ in.}^3$$

PRACTICE MAKES *PURR*-FECT™

Check your answers at BigIdeasMath.com.

Find the volume of the triangular prism. Include the units in your answer.

1.

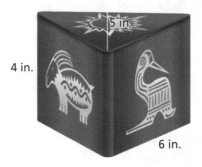

5 in.

4 in.

6 in.

$\text{Base area} = \frac{1}{2} \times$ ⬜ $\times$ ⬜

$=$ ⬜

base area   height

$\text{Volume} =$ ⬜ $\times$ ⬜ $=$ ⬜

2.

5 ft

6 ft

6 ft

$\text{Base area} = \frac{1}{2} \times$ ⬜ $\times$ ⬜

$=$ ⬜

base area   height

$\text{Volume} =$ ⬜ $\times$ ⬜ $=$ ⬜

Volume of a Cylinder

Name _____

Key Concept and Vocabulary

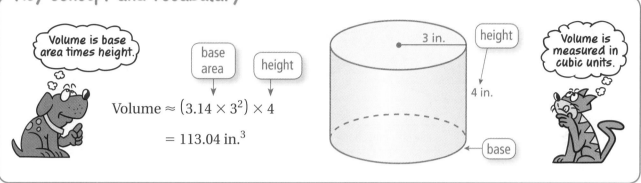

Volume is base area times height.

base area   height

Volume $\approx (3.14 \times 3^2) \times 4$

$= 113.04$ in.^{3}

3 in.

height

4 in.

base

Volume is measured in cubic units.

PRACTICE MAKES PURR-FECT™

Check your answers at BigIdeasMath.com.

Find the volume of the cylinder. Include the units in your answer.

1.

⊢—— 2 in. ——⊣

2 in.

Base area $\approx 3.14 \times$ ▭

$=$ ▭

base area   height

Volume $=$ ▭ $\times$ ▭ $=$ ▭

2.

⊢—1.5 in.—⊣

5 in.

Base area $\approx 3.14 \times$ ▭

$=$ ▭

base area   height

Volume $=$ ▭ $\times$ ▭ $=$ ▭

3. Circle the can that has the greater volume.

Congruent Figures

Name _____

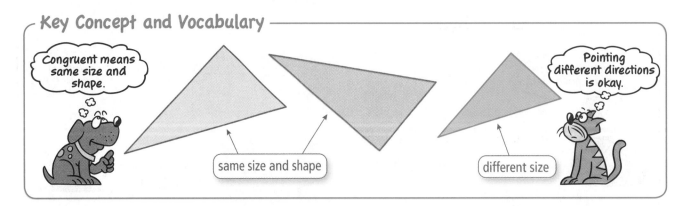
PRACTICE MAKES *PURR*-FECT™

Check your answers at BigIdeasMath.com.

Circle the two figures that are congruent.

1.

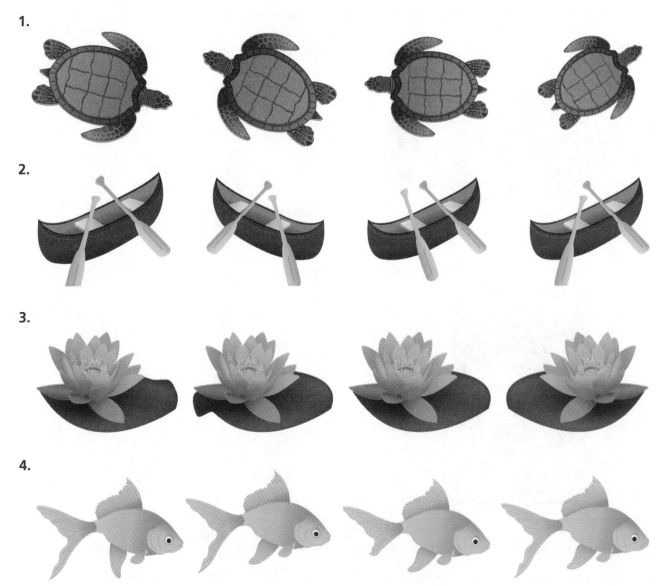

2.

3.

4.

Copyright © Big Ideas Learning, LLC

Similar Figures

Key Concept and Vocabulary

Similar figures have the same shape.

half size

full size

But, not necessarily the same size.

PRACTICE MAKES *PURR*-FECT™

Check your answers at BigIdeasMath.com.

Circle the two figures that are similar.

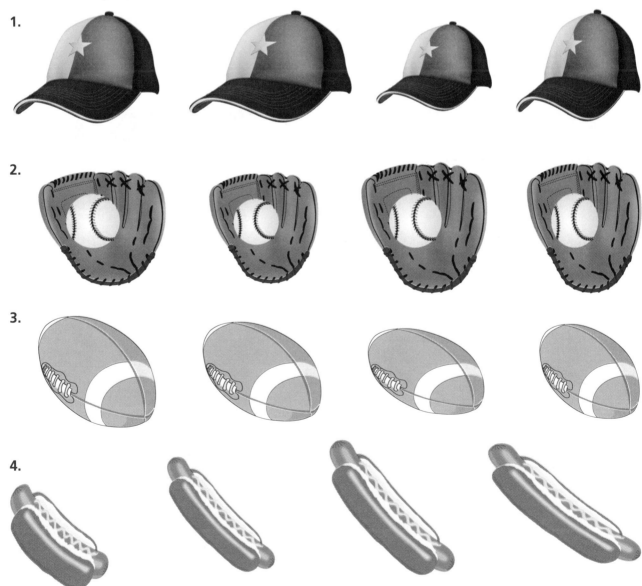

1.

2.

3.

4.

Line Symmetry

Name _____

Key Concept and Vocabulary

It's a reflection of itself.

Flip

line of reflection

When you flip it in a line, it's the same.

PRACTICE MAKES *PURR*-FECT™

Check your answers at BigIdeasMath.com.

Decide whether the figure has line symmetry. Circle the correct answer.

1.

Line Symmetry   No Line Symmetry

2.

Line Symmetry   No Line Symmetry

3.

Line Symmetry   No Line Symmetry

4.

Line Symmetry   No Line Symmetry

Rotational Symmetry

Name _____

Key Concept and Vocabulary

PRACTICE MAKES *PURR-FECT*™

Check your answers at BigIdeasMath.com.

Decide whether the figure has rotational symmetry. Circle the correct answer.

1.

| Rotational Symmetry | No Rotational Symmetry |

2.

| Rotational Symmetry | No Rotational Symmetry |

3.

| Rotational Symmetry | No Rotational Symmetry |

4.

| Rotational Symmetry | No Rotational Symmetry |

5. **FULL ROTATION** If you rotate *any* figure 360°, will it be the same?

Yes   No

Mean

Name _____

Key Concept and Vocabulary

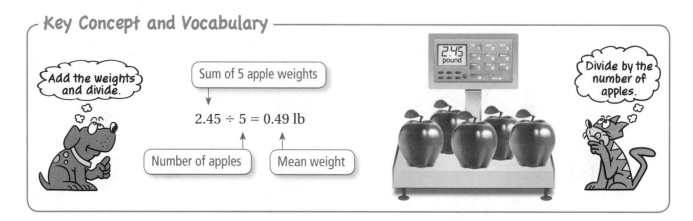

Add the weights and divide.

Sum of 5 apple weights

$2.45 \div 5 = 0.49$ lb

Number of apples

Mean weight

Divide by the number of apples.

PRACTICE MAKES *PURR*-FECT™

Check your answers at BigIdeasMath.com.

1. **LIZARD WEIGHT** Find the mean weight of the lizards. Include the units in your answer.

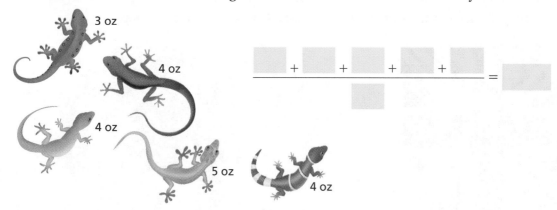

3 oz

4 oz

4 oz

5 oz

4 oz

$$\frac{\boxed{} + \boxed{} + \boxed{} + \boxed{} + \boxed{}}{\boxed{}} = \boxed{}$$

2. **GEM WIDTH** Find the mean width of the gemstones. Include the units in your answer.

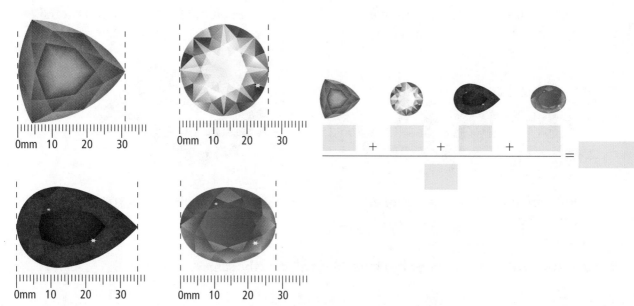

0mm 10 20 30

0mm 10 20 30

$$\frac{\boxed{} + \boxed{} + \boxed{} + \boxed{}}{\boxed{}} = \boxed{}$$

0mm 10 20 30

0mm 10 20 30

Key Concept and Vocabulary

Median

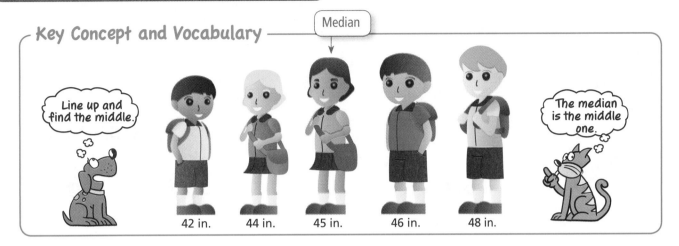

Line up and find the middle.

42 in.　44 in.　45 in.　46 in.　48 in.

The median is the middle one.

PRACTICE MAKES *PURR*-FECT™

Check your answers at BigIdeasMath.com.

1. **ODD NUMBER** Find the median horsepower of the cars.

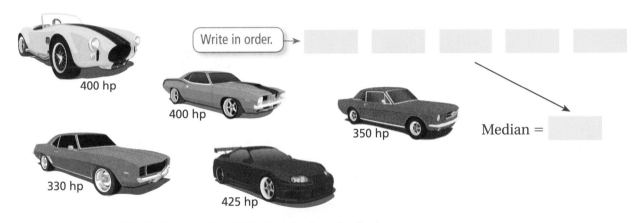

Write in order.

400 hp

400 hp

350 hp

330 hp

425 hp

Median =

2. **EVEN NUMBER** Find the median RBIs for the baseball players.

Write in order.

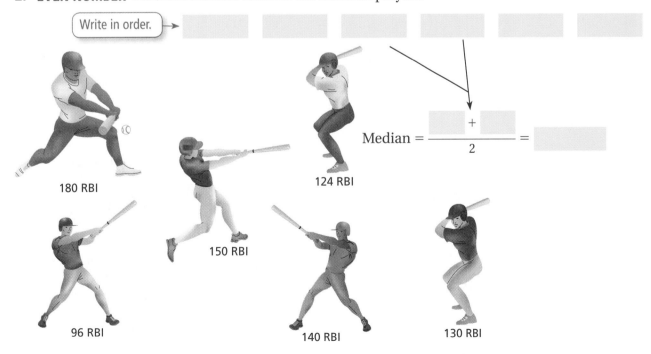

Median = $\dfrac{\boxed{} + \boxed{}}{2}$ =

180 RBI

124 RBI

150 RBI

96 RBI

140 RBI

130 RBI

Mode

Name _____

Key Concept and Vocabulary

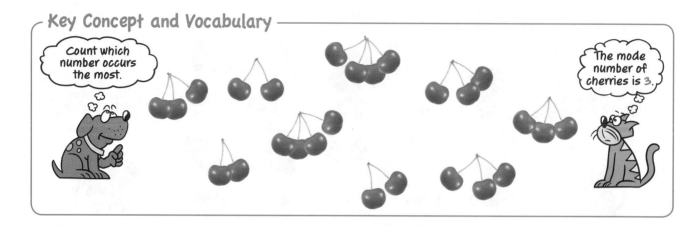

Count which number occurs the most.

The mode number of cherries is 3.

PRACTICE MAKES *PURR*-FECT™

Check your answers at BigIdeasMath.com.

1. **PROPELLERS** Find the mode number of propeller engines.

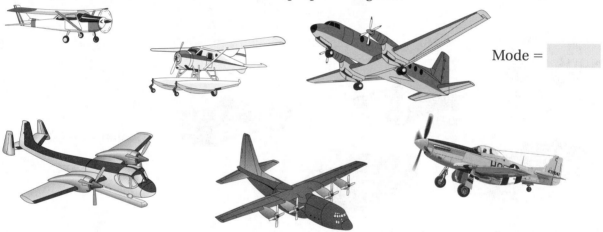

Mode = _____

2. **SALMON WEIGHTS** Find the mode of the salmon weights. Include the units in your answer.

Mode = _____

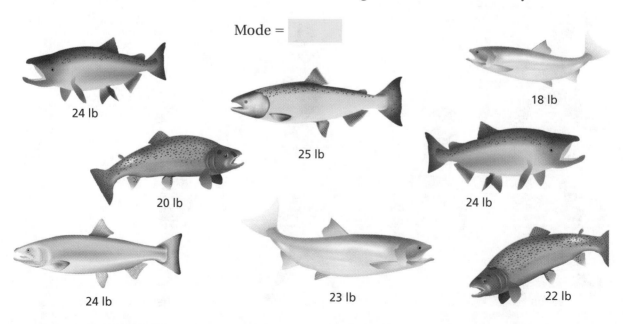

24 lb

25 lb

18 lb

20 lb

24 lb

24 lb

23 lb

22 lb

Frequency Tables

Name _____

Key Concept and Vocabulary

Tally first. Then count the tallies.

Data: 4, 6, 3, 6
4, 5, 5, 6
3, 5, 6, 3
5, 6, 6, 6

Number	Tally	Frequency
3	III	3
4	II	2
5	IIII	4
6	HHT II	7

IIII means 4.
HHT means 5.

PRACTICE MAKES *PURR*-FECT™

Check your answers at BigIdeasMath.com.

1. **PUMPKINS** Make a frequency table for the weights of the pumpkins.

6 lb 6 lb 5 lb 4 lb 4 lb
5 lb 4 lb 6 lb 6 lb 6 lb
3 lb 6 lb 5 lb 3 lb 6 lb
4 lb 3 lb 6 lb 3 lb 5 lb

Number	Tally	Frequency
3		
4		
5		
6		

2. **DAIRY COWS** Make a frequency table for the ages (in years) of the dairy cows.

Data: 2, 2, 3, 4, 5, 6, 2, 3, 7, 6, 3, 3, 4, 2, 5, 5, 7
6, 3, 5, 6, 3, 5, 6, 6, 4, 5, 2, 3, 2, 4, 4, 3, 2

Number	Tally	Frequency
2		
3		
4		
5		
6		
7		

Bar Graphs

Name _____

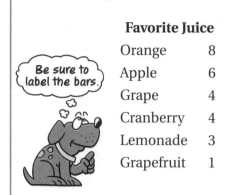

Favorite Juice

Orange	8
Apple	6
Grape	4
Cranberry	4
Lemonade	3
Grapefruit	1

Be sure to label the bars.

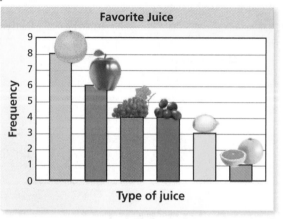

The bar height shows how many chose each juice.

PRACTICE MAKES *PURR*-FECT™

Check your answers at BigIdeasMath.com.

1. **FAVORITE AFRICAN ANIMALS** Make a bar graph showing the results of the survey.

Elephant: 8

Giraffe: 6

Zebra: 4

Lion: 10

Baboon: 2

Cheetah: 9

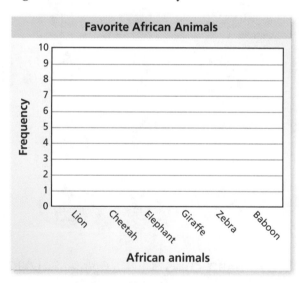

2. **AMUSEMENT PARK RIDES** How many people were surveyed about their favorite amusement park ride?

Number in survey = [ ] people

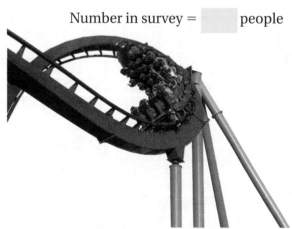

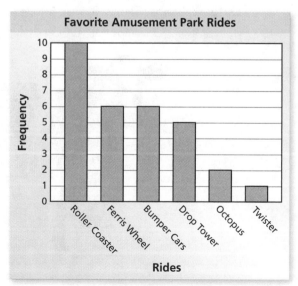

Double Bar Graphs

Name _____

Key Concept and Vocabulary

Two data sets are compared.

Total Points in a Season

	Team A	Team B
2010	50	90
2011	60	70
2012	70	50
2013	80	30

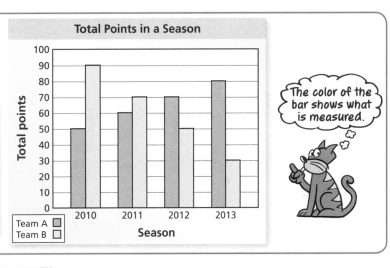

The color of the bar shows what is measured.

PRACTICE MAKES *PURR*-FECT™

Check your answers at BigIdeasMath.com.

1. **COMPARING HOCKEY TEAMS** Make a double bar graph that compares the two teams.

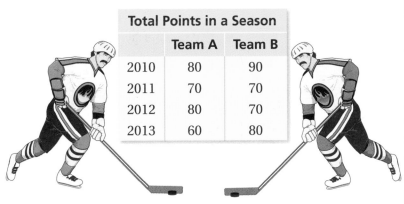

Total Points in a Season

	Team A	Team B
2010	80	90
2011	70	70
2012	80	70
2013	60	80

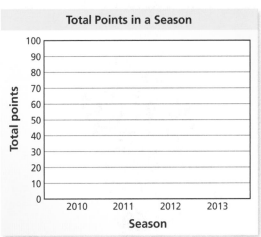

2. **POLAR BEARS AND SEALS** Estimate the population of each animal in 2011.

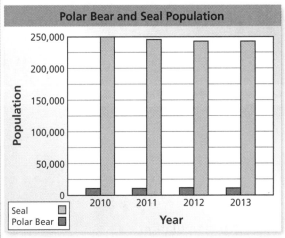

Line Graphs

Name _____

Key Concept and Vocabulary

Line graphs show change over time.

	Savings Balance
2010	$100
2011	$160
2012	$200
2013	$300
2014	$450

The horizontal axis shows the time.

PRACTICE MAKES *PURR*-FECT™

Check your answers at BigIdeasMath.com.

1. **SAVINGS ACCOUNT** Make a line graph that shows the balance in the savings account.

	Savings Balance
2009	$200
2010	$250
2011	$400
2012	$450
2013	$650
2014	$950

2. **POPULATION OF CANADA** Find the population of Canada in 1960 and in 2000.

1960 Population

2000 Population

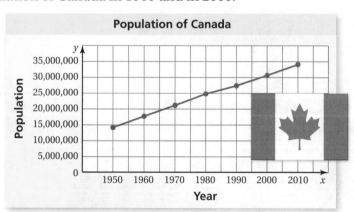

Circle Graphs

Key Concept and Vocabulary

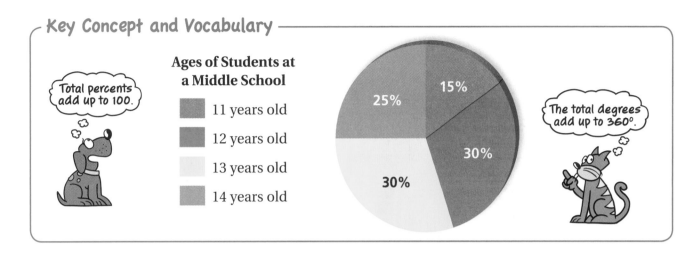

Total percents add up to 100.

Ages of Students at a Middle School

- 11 years old
- 12 years old
- 13 years old
- 14 years old

15%
25%
30%
30%

The total degrees add up to 360°.

PRACTICE MAKES *PURR*-FECT™

Check your answers at BigIdeasMath.com.

1. **FAVORITE CLASS** Make a circle graph that shows the favorite class in middle school.

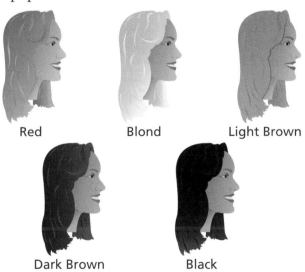

Language Arts:	5%
Math:	30%
Science:	20%
Social Studies:	15%
Physical Education:	10%
Art:	20%

2. **HAIR COLOR** Estimate the percent of the population with each hair color.

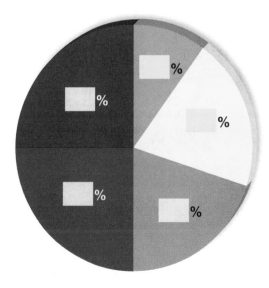

Red   Blond   Light Brown

Dark Brown   Black

____%
____%
____%
____%
____%

Pictographs

Name _____

Number of Baskets Made in a Game

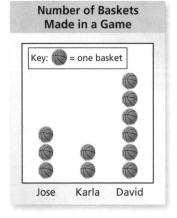

Each basketball represents the number of baskets made in a game.

Key: = one basket

Jose   Karla   David

David made 6 baskets, which is the most.

PRACTICE MAKES *PURR-FECT*™

Check your answers at BigIdeasMath.com.

Use the pictograph at the right.

1. Which day had the most number of hot dogs sold?

2. Which day had the least number of hot dogs sold?

3. Which days sold the same number of hot dogs?

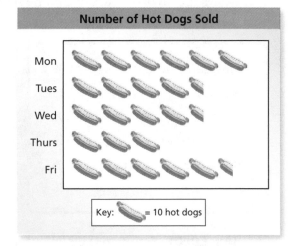

Number of Hot Dogs Sold

Mon
Tues
Wed
Thurs
Fri

Key: = 10 hot dogs

4. How many hot dogs were sold on each day?

    Monday ___   Tuesday ___   Wednesday ___   Thursday ___   Friday ___

5. Create a pictograph that shows the number of songs downloaded.

Number of Songs Downloaded	
Week	**Songs**
1	4
2	7
3	6
4	4

Name _____

Key Concept and Vocabulary

A pint is a pound the world around.

Length	Weight	Volume
1 ft = 12 in.	1 lb = 16 oz	1 cup = 8 fl oz
1 yd = 3 ft	1 ton = 2000 lb	1 pt = 2 cups
1 mi = 5280 ft		1 qt = 2 pts
		1 gal = 4 qt

There are two types of ounces.

PRACTICE MAKES *PURR*-FECT™

Check your answers at BigIdeasMath.com.

1. VOLUME Label the drink containers as *cup, pint, quart, half gallon,* or *gallon*.

2. VOLUME How many fluid ounces are in each size? Describe the pattern.

Cup = _____ fl oz

Pint = _____ fl oz

Quart = _____ fl oz

Half gallon = _____ fl oz

Gallon = _____ fl oz

Pattern:

3. FOOTBALL FIELD Find the length and width of the football field in feet.

Length = _____ ft   Width = _____ ft

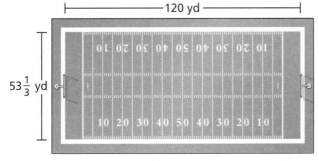

120 yd

$53\frac{1}{3}$ yd

4. PICKUP TRUCK Find the weight of the pickup truck in pounds.

Weight = _____ lb

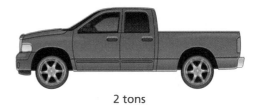

2 tons

Converting Metric Units

Name _____

Key Concept and Vocabulary

100 centimeters in a meter

Length	Weight	Volume
1 cm = 10 mm	1 g = 1000 mg	1 L = 1000 mL
1 m = 100 cm	1 kg = 1000 g	1 kL = 1000 L
1 km = 1000 m		

10 millimeters in a centimeter

PRACTICE MAKES *PURR-FECT*™

Check your answers at BigIdeasMath.com.

1. **WORD MEANING** Write the meaning of "*kilo.*"

   1 *kilo*meter = [   ] meters

   1 *kilo*gram = [   ] grams

   1 *kilo*liter = [   ] liters

   "*kilo*" means [   ]

2. **LITER AND QUART** Which is more, a liter or a quart? Circle the correct answer.

   | Liter is more. | Quart is more. |

3. **KILOMETER AND MILE** Which takes longer, driving a kilometer or a mile? Circle the correct answer.

   Kilometer takes longer.

   Mile takes longer.

   |———————— 8 kilometers ————————|

   |———————— 5 miles ————————|

4. **KILOGRAM AND POUND** Which is more, a kilogram or a pound? Circle the correct answer.

   Kilogram is more.

   Pound is more.

   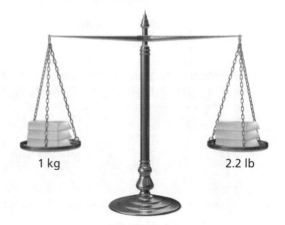

   1 kg   2.2 lb

Using a Compass

Name _____

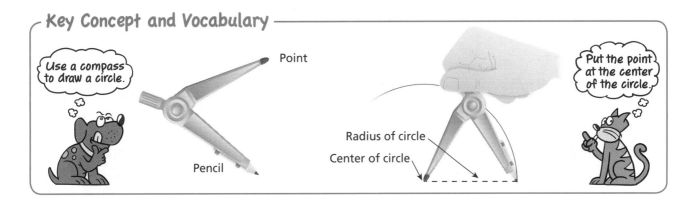
PRACTICE MAKES *PURR-FECT*™

Check your answers at BigIdeasMath.com.

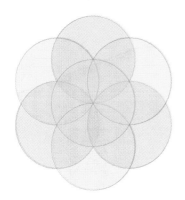

1. CIRCLE DESIGN Use a compass to complete the circle design. Color your design. Keep each radius the same.

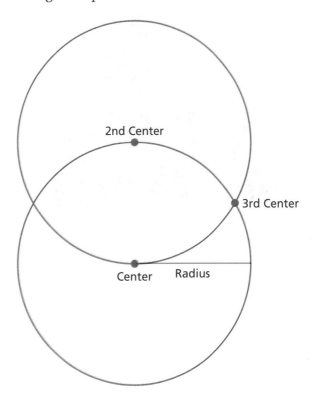

Using a Protractor

Name _____

Protractors have two sets of angles.

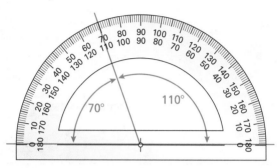

70°   110°

Decide which set to use by comparing to 90°.

PRACTICE MAKES *PURR*-FECT™

Check your answers at BigIdeasMath.com.

Use a protractor to measure the angle.

1.

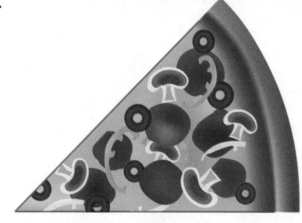

_____ °

2.

_____ °

3.

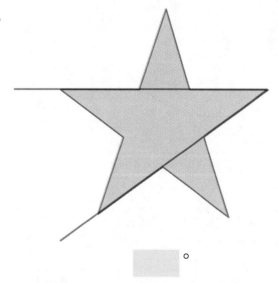

_____ °

4.

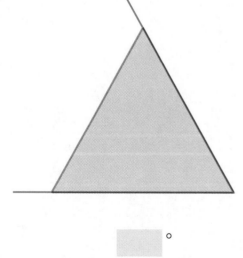

_____ °

Evaluating Formulas

Name _____

Key Concept and Vocabulary

Distance equals rate times time.

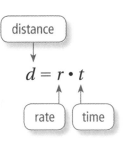

distance

$$d = r \cdot t$$

rate   time

Rate = 60 mi/h
Time = 2 h

rate   time

Distance = $60 \dfrac{mi}{h} \cdot 2 \cancel{h}$

= 120 mi

The rate of a car is its speed.

PRACTICE MAKES *PURR*-FECT™

Check your answers at BigIdeasMath.com.

1. **AMBULANCE** The ambulance driver needs to drive 5 miles in 5 minutes. How fast should the driver drive?

$$5 \text{ min} = \dfrac{\square}{60} \text{ h}$$

time

rate

$$5 \text{ mi} = \square \dfrac{mi}{h} \cdot \dfrac{\square}{60} \text{ h}$$

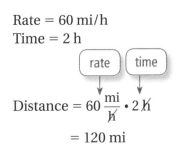

AMBULANCE

2. **FIRE TRUCK** The firefighter needs to drive 3 miles in 3 minutes. How fast should the firefighter drive?

$$3 \text{ min} = \dfrac{\square}{60} \text{ h}$$

time

rate

$$3 \text{ mi} = \square \dfrac{mi}{h} \cdot \dfrac{\square}{60} \text{ h}$$

Making Tables

Name _____

PRACTICE MAKES *PURR*-FECT™

Check your answers at BigIdeasMath.com.

1. **TEMPERATURE CONVERSION** Complete the table.

Celsius, C	0°	5°	10°	15°	20°	25°	30°
Fahrenheit, F					68°		

Freezing

2. **BOILING WATER** Water boils at 212° Fahrenheit. At what temperature does water boil in Celsius?

$$212 = \frac{9}{5} \cdot \boxed{} + 32$$

Boiling, F   Boiling, C

Describing Patterns

Name _____

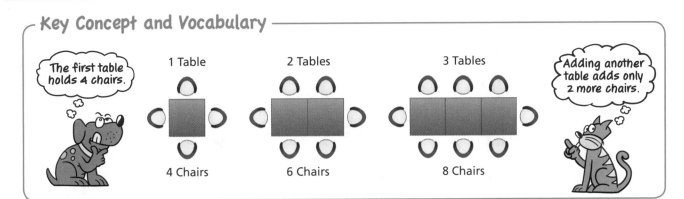

The first table holds 4 chairs.

1 Table
4 Chairs

2 Tables
6 Chairs

3 Tables
8 Chairs

Adding another table adds only 2 more chairs.

PRACTICE MAKES *PURR*-FECT™

Check your answers at BigIdeasMath.com.

1. **EXTENDING A PATTERN** Complete the table.

Number of Tables	1	2	3	4	5	6	7
Number of Chairs	4	6	8				

2. **FLOWER PETALS** Complete the table.

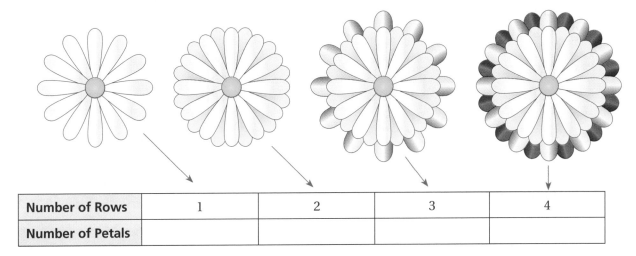

Number of Rows	1	2	3	4
Number of Petals				

Drawing a Graph

Name _____

Key Concept and Vocabulary

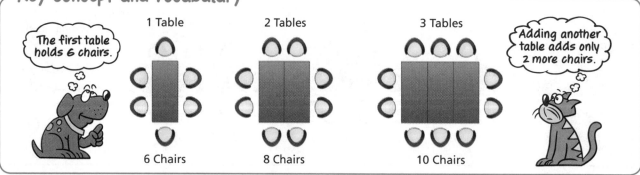

PRACTICE MAKES *PURR*-FECT™

Check your answers at BigIdeasMath.com.

1. **EXTENDING A PATTERN** Complete the table.

Tables	1	2	3	4	5	6	7
Chairs	6	8	10				

2. **GRAPHING A PATTERN** Complete the graph.

3. **DESCRIBING A PATTERN** Describe the pattern of the graph.

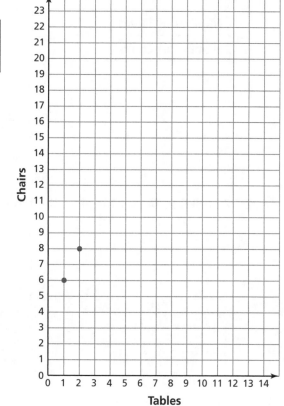

4. **EXTENDING A PATTERN** If you set up 10 tables, how many chairs would there be?

_____ chairs

Sequences

Name _____

Key Concept and Vocabulary

A **sequence** is a series of numbers. Each number in a sequence is called a **term**. You can identify patterns to find missing terms of a sequence.

Each term is 2 more than the previous term.

Sequence:

3, 5, 7, 9, ?, ?, . . .

+2 +2 +2 +2 +2

Fifth term: 9 + 2 = 11
Sixth term: 11 + 2 = 13

PRACTICE MAKES *PURR-FECT*™

Check your answers at BigIdeasMath.com.

Find the sixth term of the sequence.

1. 0, 1, 2, 3, . . .

2. 100, 90, 80, 70, . . .

3. 8, 16, 32, 64, . . .

4. $9, 3, 1, \dfrac{1}{3}, \ldots$

Find the tenth term of the sequence.

5. 9.2, 8.8, 8.4, 8.0, . . .

6. $\dfrac{1}{2}, \dfrac{3}{2}, \dfrac{5}{2}, \dfrac{7}{2}, \ldots$

7. 256, 128, 64, 32, . . .

8. $\dfrac{1}{25}, \dfrac{1}{5}, 1, 5, \ldots$

9. PAY RATE Your boss pays you $0.03 the first day you work, $0.06 the second day, $0.12 the third day, $0.24 the fourth day, and so on. How much do you earn on the seventh day? fourteenth day?

10. BACTERIA The table shows the number of bacteria in a sample for consecutive hours. Write the first eight terms of the sequence for the population. Interpret the eighth term.

Time	1 P.M.	2 P.M.	3 P.M.	4 P.M.
Bacteria	10	100	1000	10,000

Evaluating Expressions

Name _____

PRACTICE MAKES *PURR*-FECT™

Check your answers at BigIdeasMath.com.

1. You have 74 songs on your MP3 player and you want to download 12 more songs. How many songs will you have on your MP3 player after you download the new songs?

   Visual Model:

   Expression:

   Solution:

2. There are 48 minutes in a basketball game in the NBA. If 35 minutes have gone by, how much time is remaining in the game?

   Visual Model:

   Expression:

   Solution:

Copyright © Big Ideas Learning, LLC

Function Rules

Name _____

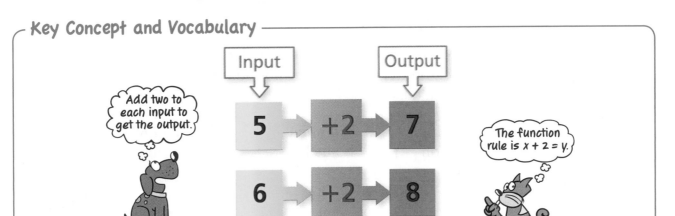

PRACTICE MAKES *PURR-FECT*™

Check your answers at BigIdeasMath.com.

Identify the function rule.

1.

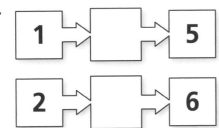

The function rule is _____ .

2.

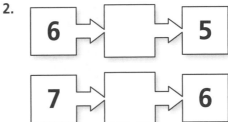

The function rule is _____ .

3.

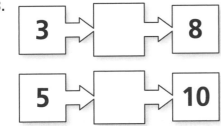

The function rule is _____ .

4.

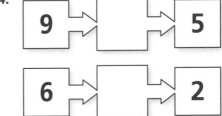

The function rule is _____ .

Name _____

Key Concept and Vocabulary

Use the information to write an expression.

Joe worked four more hours than Jackson. If Jackson worked six hours, how many hours did Joe work?

Number of hours Jackson worked	+	Additional hours Joe worked	=	Number of hours Joe worked
6	+	4	=	10

So, Joe worked 10 hours.

"more" means add.

PRACTICE MAKES *PURR*-FECT™

Check your answers at BigIdeasMath.com.

1. You have sixteen CDs and thirteen DVDs. How many more CDs do you have than DVDs?

2. You have two hundred eleven friends on Facebook and your sister has four hundred sixty-two friends on Facebook. Who has more friends on Facebook? How many more?

3. The table shows your cell phone bill for one month. How much do you spend on your cell phone in one month?

Unlimited Calling	$43
Unlimited Text Messaging	$12

4. You and your friend raised money for charity by collecting money and participating in a five-mile walk. You collected one hundred twenty dollars and your friend collected two hundred thirty-five dollars. Who collected more money? How much more?

5. You have eighty-two songs on your MP3 player. If you add twenty-one more songs, how many songs are on your MP3 player?

6. Your goal is to swim three hundred yards in the pool. You have fifty-five yards until you meet your goal. How many yards have you already swam?

Ratios

Name _____

Key Concept and Vocabulary

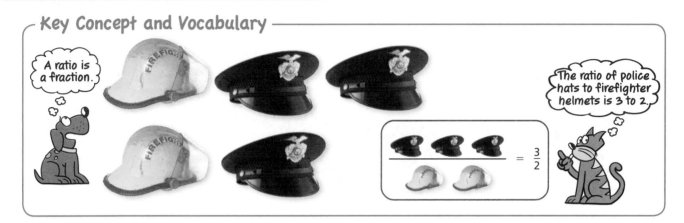

A ratio is a fraction.

The ratio of police hats to firefighter helmets is 3 to 2.

$$= \frac{3}{2}$$

PRACTICE MAKES *PURR*-FECT™

Check your answers at BigIdeasMath.com.

1. **WRITING A RATIO** Write the ratio of Army helmets to Navy caps. Simplify your answer.

Ratio = _____

Simplified Ratio = _____

2. **WRITING A RATIO** Write the ratio of Navy caps to Army helmets. Simplify your answer.

Ratio = _____   Simplified Ratio = _____

3. **WRITING A RATIO** Write the ratio of football helmets to baseball caps. Simplify your answer.

Ratio = _____

Simplified Ratio = _____

Rates

Name _____

PRACTICE MAKES *PURR*-FECT™

Check your answers at BigIdeasMath.com.

Find the rate and the unit rate.

1.

Earns $200 in eight hours.

Rate = _____

Unit Rate = _____

2.

Earns $1600 in forty hours.

Rate = _____

Unit Rate = _____

3.

Earns $800 in eighty hours.

Rate = _____

Unit Rate = _____

4.

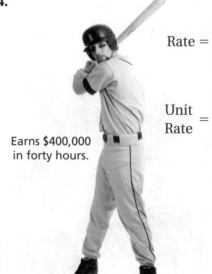

Earns $400,000 in forty hours.

Rate = _____

Unit Rate = _____

Proportions

Name _____

A proportion equates two ratios or two rates.

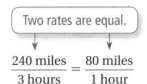

Two rates are equal.

$$\frac{240 \text{ miles}}{3 \text{ hours}} = \frac{80 \text{ miles}}{1 \text{ hour}}$$

Motorcyclist

Use "per" when reading a rate. 80 miles per hour.

PRACTICE MAKES *PURR*-FECT™

Check your answers at BigIdeasMath.com.

Decide whether the two rates are equal. Write = or ≠ in ☐. Circle the correct answer.

1.

Horse

Proportion

Not a Proportion

$$\frac{15 \text{ miles}}{0.5 \text{ hour}} \qquad \frac{30 \text{ miles}}{1 \text{ hour}}$$

2.

Bicyclist

Proportion

Not a Proportion

$$\frac{200 \text{ miles}}{10 \text{ hours}} \qquad \frac{25 \text{ miles}}{1 \text{ hour}}$$

3.

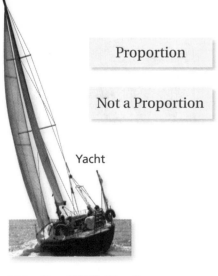

Proportion

Not a Proportion

Yacht

$$\frac{250 \text{ miles}}{5 \text{ hours}} \qquad \frac{50 \text{ miles}}{1 \text{ hour}}$$

4.

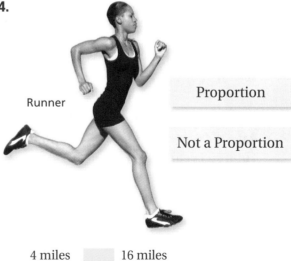

Runner

Proportion

Not a Proportion

$$\frac{4 \text{ miles}}{0.25 \text{ hour}} \qquad \frac{16 \text{ miles}}{1 \text{ hour}}$$

Simple Interest

Name _____

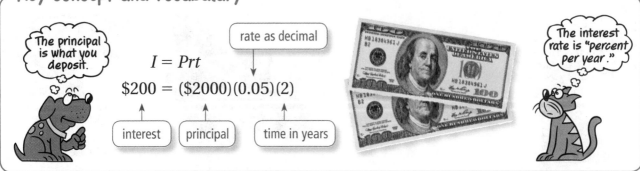

The principal is what you deposit.

rate as decimal

$I = Prt$

$200 = ($2000)(0.05)(2)$

interest principal time in years

The interest rate is "percent per year."

PRACTICE MAKES *PURR*-FECT™

Check your answers at BigIdeasMath.com.

1. **TIME IN YEARS** Complete the table.

1 month	3 months	4 months	6 months	1 year	2 years
$t =$	$t =$	$t =$	$t =$	$t =$	$t =$

2. **RATE AS A DECIMAL** Complete the table.

3% per yr	4% per yr	5% per yr	6% per yr	6.5% per yr	10% per yr
$r =$	$r =$	$r =$	$r =$	$r =$	$r =$

Find the interest earned in the savings account.

3. Principal = $2000
   Rate = 5% per year
   Time = 6 months

   $I = $ _____

4. Principal = $2000
   Rate = 6% per year
   Time = 6 months

   $I = $ _____

5. Principal = $10,000
   Rate = 4% per year
   Time = 6 years

   $I = $ _____

6. Principal = $10,000
   Rate = 6% per year
   Time = 6 years

   $I = $ _____

Comparing Rates

Name _____

Key Concept and Vocabulary

Motorcyclist

Compare the numerators if you have a common denominator.

60 is less than 80.

$$\frac{60 \text{ miles}}{1 \text{ hour}} < \frac{80 \text{ miles}}{1 \text{ hour}}$$

So, the speed of the motorcyclist is faster.

Because < is used, the second rate is faster than the first rate.

PRACTICE MAKES *PURR*-FECT™

Check your answers at BigIdeasMath.com.

1.

Horse

Faster

Slower

$$\frac{50 \text{ miles}}{1 \text{ hour}} \qquad \frac{30 \text{ miles}}{1 \text{ hour}}$$

2.

Bicyclist

Faster

Slower

$$\frac{24 \text{ miles}}{1 \text{ hour}} \qquad \frac{25 \text{ miles}}{1 \text{ hour}}$$

3.

Yacht

$$\frac{75 \text{ miles}}{1 \text{ hour}} \qquad \frac{50 \text{ miles}}{1 \text{ hour}}$$

Faster

Slower

4.

Runner

Faster

Slower

$$\frac{1.6 \text{ miles}}{1 \text{ hour}} \qquad \frac{16 \text{ miles}}{1 \text{ hour}}$$

Photo Credits

33 ©iStockphoto.com/o-che; 44 *Exercise 4* ©iStockphoto.com/
borisyankov; *Exercise 7* ©iStockphoto.com/sndr; 45 *Exercise 4*
©iStockphoto.com/borisyankov; 49 ©iStockphoto.com/Vallentin;
52 ©iStockphoto.com/Vallentin; 54 ©iStockphoto.com/Photozek07;
58 *Exercise 10a* Greg Williams; 65 *Exercise 5* ©iStockphoto.com/
jacomstephens; 85 *Exercise 5* ©iStockphoto.com/sweetym; 91 *Exercise 1*
Four Oaks, ©iStockphoto.com/DaddyBit, Kletr; 97 Christos Georghiou;
107 ©iStockphoto.com/MychkoAlezander; 115 *bottom right 1* Rob
Wilson; *bottom right 2* ©iStockphoto.com/bsauter; *bottom right 3*
Big Ideas Learning, LLC; 116 LouLouPhotos; 117 ©iStockphoto.com/
LUGO; 120 *bottom left* ©iStockphoto.com/procurator;
127 *cardinal* Ron Waldrop; *dove* Robert Taylor; *robin* gregg williams;
128 Eric Isselée, ©iStockphoto.com/LivingImages, ©iStockphoto.com/
salihguler, ©iStockphoto.com/Mehmet Salih Guler;
130 ©iStockphoto.com/ShaneKato; 133 ©iStockphoto.com/mladn61;
136 werg; 137 Dusty Cline; 140 *Exercise 1* User Greverod on sv.wikipedia;
Exercise 2 Alex//Berlin (Stay in Madrid); *Exercise 3* ©iStockphoto.com/
LUke1138; *Exercise 4* bukitdamansara; *Exercise 5* ©iStockphoto.com/
Yails; *Exercise 6* ©iStockphoto.com/corsicasmart; 150 *top*
©iStockphoto.com/magnetcreative; 152 *top* ©iStockphoto.com/
procurator; 153 *Exercise 1* ©iStockphoto.com/schlol;
155 ©iStockphoto.com/Hanis; 156 *top* ©iStockphoto.com/procurator,
©iStockphoto.com/vladars; *Exercise 1* Four Oaks, ©iStockphoto.com/
DaddyBit, Kletr, Eric Isselée; *Exercise 2* ©iStockphoto.com/
AndreasWeber; 157 *Exercise 2* Andreas Meyer, Taily; 158 Big Ideas
Learning, LLC; 161 *Exercise 4* ©iStockphoto.com/sunygraphics;
162 ©iStockphoto.com/biosurf; 166 ©iStockphoto.com/joebelanger;
172 *Exercise 1* ©iStockphoto.com/borisyankov; *Exercise 6*
©iStockphoto.com/ShaneKato; 173 *top* Cheryl Casey, Katrina Brown;
Exercise 1 EchoArt, Dani Simmonds; *Exercise 3* Nicholas Piccillo,
jamalludin; 174 *top* Lisa F. Young; *Exercise 1* Stephen Cobum;
Exercise 2 Kurhan; *Exercise 3* James Steidl; *Exercise 4* Nicholas Piccillo;
175 *top* fenlan1976; *Exercise 1* Benjamin F. Haith; *Exercise 2* Vaclav
Volrab; *Exercise 3* Taiga; *Exercise 4* ©iStockphoto.com/jacomstephens;
176 *top* grocap; *bottom* Denis Vrublevski; 177 *top* fenlan1976; *Exercise 1*
©iStockphoto.com/gapwedge; *Exercise 2* ©iStockphoto.com/RapidEye;
Exercise 3 ©iStockphoto.com/dan_prat; *Exercise 4* ©iStockphoto.com/
leezsnow

Cartoon illustrations Tyler Stout